S/ ΛE

S/HE

Minnie Bruce Pratt

A Sapphic Classic from
Sinister Wisdom

Sinister Wisdom, Inc.
2333 McIntosh Road
Dover, FL 33527
sinisterwisdom@gmail.com
www.sinisterwisdom.org

Designed by Nieves Guerra.
Transcription by Bell Pitkin.
Copyedit and review by Ivy Marie
        and Taylor Marie Doherty.

Cover photograph, Minnie Bruce Pratt
© Marilyn Humphries 2024. Used with Permission.

First edition, December 2024

ISBN-13: 978-1944981761

Printed in the U.S. on recycled paper.

For Leslie, my one and only *you.*

CONTENTS

GENDER QUIZ

Quiz, n. [? suggested by L. *quis*, who, which, what, *quid*, how, why, wherefore]. 1. [Rare], a queer or eccentric person; 2. a practical joke; 3. a questioning, especially an informal oral or written examination to test one's knowledge.

Webster's New World Dictionary
of the American Language

In 1975, when I first fell in love with another woman, and knew that was what I was doing, I was married to a man, had been for almost ten years, and I had two small sons. Everyone was shocked at the turn I was taking in my life, including me. Everyone—from the male lawyer who handled the divorce to my handful of lesbian friends—wanted to know: Had I ever had these feelings before? When had I realized I was "different"? When had I started to "change"? And the state of North Carolina, where I was living, certainly wanted to know: Did I understand that I could not be both a mother—a good woman—and also a lesbian—a perverted woman?

To answer their questions and my own, I did what perhaps every person who identifies as lesbian or gay does when we come out to ourselves. I looked back at my own life for the clues of memory to use as I struggled through a maze of questions: I didn't feel "different," but was I? (From who?) Had I changed? (From what?) Was I heterosexual in adolescence only to become a lesbian in my late twenties? Was I lesbian always but coerced into heterosexuality? Was I a less authentic lesbian than my friends who had "always known" that they were sexually and affectionately attracted to other women? What kind of woman was a lesbian woman? Was I a "real" woman?

What I found at the center of my exploration was my first friendship, when I was five and she was five, with a white girl who lived next door to me, a tomboy. I had not talked to her since our high school graduation in our small Alabama town, but I knew from my mother that she had never married. I wondered at how intensely I remembered her. Then one evening, as I read my poetry in a Birmingham bookstore, she walked in, looking grown and fine in her cowboy boots, white shirt open at the collar, tailored slacks—looking like the butch dyke she had turned out to be. She was someone who had known me since I was small, but she was as shocked as everyone else that I had grown up to be a lesbian too.

When I found her, I found other questions that required me to turn back and look yet again: How was it possible that coming from the woman-hating, race-baiting, church town of our childhood, we had both grown to live as lesbians? Why was she the first person I felt passionately about outside my family—someone who was not only a lesbian, but a butch lesbian? How had we recognized each other then, with no language for who we were? What mark had we left on the other? And who *were* we to each other, at five years old? Were we "butch" and "femme"? Were we "boy" and "girl"? Why was I invisible in her memories, a "girl" but not a "lesbian"?

I turned and looked back again at the two of us, those two girls. I saw the kite string slack in my hand, the kite falling and crumpling, and how she reached out and pulled me forward into the wind with it. I said to her, "But after we were little, I never saw you. You were always playing with the boys. I was afraid of the boys." And she said, "But what you didn't know was that I was afraid of the girls." All through high school she fell miserably in love with straight girls who were agressively femme, but at the senior prom she dated the captain of the football team. I sat sedate, awkward, and alone in a strapless pink prom dress, full of anticipated power but unable to sail into a room of dancers who, like me, desired and despised the power of women.

Twenty years later these questions unwound before me: Was my femme style—the tilt of my head, my way of asking questions, the tone of my voice—related to my sexual desire? To my notion of myself as a woman? What did maleness and femaleness have to do with the identities of butch and femme we had grown up into? What did the gestures of masculinity and femininity have to do with us as women?

The next time I came home she arranged another reunion, a dinner with queer folks from our high school years. That night there were five, all of us white, a friendship network as segregated as our education, our never even getting to meet the Black students in the school on the other side of town. We hadn't known much about many of the lives hidden in our town, and now we gathered, ready to find out: Me and the woman who was my first friend, almost my first memory. And my best girlfriend from high school, who'd also grown up to be a lesbian and a mother. My first boyfriend, who'd turned out to be a gay man so sweet I remembered why I wanted to be his girl. And another gay man who still lived in our hometown. We gossiped about who we'd had crushes on, who we held hands with on the sly, who flirted back.

The list of people became staggeringly long, far beyond my idea of who might have been "lesbian" or "gay" in my tiny town of about two thousand. There was the girl classmate, long since married, who'd graduated and then had an affair with the woman gym teacher. And the girl classmate who had gone from one woman lover to another until her front door got broken down in the middle of the night. And the married Sunday School teacher whose daughter, later married, had had an affair with a girlfriend, who years later had had an affair with the teacher-mother. There were the boys who either did it with each other or watched the fucking that went on between them in a church, in a parsonage, with the preacher's son. There was a gay man who opened his door one night to find an envelope on his doorstep stuffed with photographs of a married male acquaintance, with a pleading invitation.

We told stories about taking the compulsory heterosexual quiz in high school, with its two ways to answer, its two ways to turn: straight or gay, heterosexual or queer. One choice would lead us out of the maze into adulthood, the other directly to hell. But it seemed that the public tally of our choices had almost no relation to our hidden lives, to whose hand was on whose ass, to the dream we buried, dead center, in our heart. The institution of heterosexuality certainly existed, but its daily practice—at least in my hometown in the Deep South—suddenly seemed no more sturdy than the wedding pictures of man and wife printed on flimsy yellow paper in the local weekly.

Yet law and custom had usually been strong enough to make our public lives match the picture. The boundaries of heterosexuality strengthened other institutions—including those of race and class—whose limits were also unacknowledged. In the town newspaper I saw photographs of the sheriff and his deputies by the courthouse, pouring confiscated whiskey into the street gutters until the town reeked of moonshine. But there were no pictures of my girlfriend inside her house, on her hands and knees in the kitchen with a mother almost broken by poverty. No picture of her father jailed for trying to buy their way out by selling bootleg liquor. When my white father died in the county nursing home, the paper printed one version of his life, from semi-pro baseball to the lumber mill. No mention of him drinking the bootleg whiskey, no mention of his racist theories on who was taking over the world. The Black woman who raised me died across the hall from him in the home. There was nothing in the paper to say she had lived or died, or how many children she had mothered, nothing of her daughters or grandchildren.

When I was engaged to be married to a man, the local paper published an announcement and a picture of me, groomed and womanly, ready to be a wife. Of those of us gathered at our queer reunion, there was no public record in our town—no note in the weekly chat column from Greenpond or Six Mile—of those we had loved faithfully for five years, ten years, the children we had familied. But in our bodies we knew that our way had not led to a dead end, a blank wall, a blank piece of paper. We had walked through into our own lives.

The last time I went home, I introduced my new love to my first girlfriend and watched them greet each other warmly.

After years of loving butch lesbians, I had taken as my mate a woman so stone in her masculinity that she could, and did, sometimes pass as a queer man. I had no language to talk about her or us together. I had to learn to say that I had fallen in love with a woman so *transgendered*, with such perceived contradictions between her birth sex and her gender expression, that someone at one end of the city block would call her "Ma'am" and someone at the other end would call her "Sir." I was learning that I was more complicated than I'd had any idea. I was beginning to pull the thread of who *I* was out of the tangle of words: *woman* and *lesbian, femme* and *female.*

That night I looked back at my first friend, a girl scalded by her mother's shame. The threats of walk-like-a-lady, of don't-be-so-loud-and-angry. (And hate yourself enough to almost go crazy.) I looked back at myself, the child flirting in photographs with angled head, sidelong glance. The child given an impossible choice by her teachers: Be smart or be a girl, be a girl or be strong. (And hate yourself enough to almost leave your body.) The two of us had sat at playtime in the dirt, barefoot, battling furiously hand-to-hand in the desire to defeat the other. How had we survived to meet again? Survived to grow up to be women for whom the word woman did not adequately describe the twists and turns our bodies, our lives, took through sex and gender?

No one had turned to us and held out a handful of questions: How many ways are there to have the *sex* of girl, boy, man, woman? How many ways are there to have *gender*—from masculine to androgynous to feminine? Is there a connection between the *sexualities* of lesbian, bisexual, heterosexual, between desire and liberation? No one told us: The path divides, and divides again, in many directions. No one asked: How many ways can the *body's sex* vary by chromosomes, hormones, genitals? How many ways can *gender expression* multiply—between home and work, at the computer and when you kiss someone, in your dreams and when you walk down the street? No one asked us: What is your dream of who you want to be?

In 1975, when I first fell in love with another woman, and knew that was what I wanted, I had just begun to call myself a feminist. I was learning how many traps the female body could be caught in—sexual assault and rape, beatings in the home, our thoughts turned back in shame on our bodies. I learned how women's bodies could be used to reproduce children without our consent, to produce someone else's "pleasure" at our expense. Most importantly, I began to be able to explain many of the events of my own life that had been unintelligible to me.

I was able to recall and find a pattern in certain acts that had made no sense—like a sexually suggestive comment from a male co-worker—and acts that I hadn't understood as significant—such as the fact that the male job interviewer questioned me on my childcare arrangements. For the first time in my life, I understood myself as *woman*, the "opposite sex," a group of people subject to discrimination and oppression—and capable of resistance. I was able to locate my body and my life in the maze of history and power.

The oppression of women was a revelation to me; the liberation of women was my freedom. There was tremendous exhilaration in being part of a liberation movement, in gathering together with other women to explore how to get freedom. In consciousness-raising circles, political action groups, cultural events, literary collectives—in all kinds of women's groups and spaces, we identified the ways oppression had fenced in our lives.

And we read the theories of women who had ideas about how to end the oppression of women as a sex. I found a few writers who examined the relation of capitalist economic development to women's oppression. But most of the theory available to me was ahistorical and monocultural. It emphasized that the solution was to eliminate differences between *women* and *men*. Some proposed abolishing distinctions in biological functioning—as in Shulamith Firestone's suggestion for artificial wombs to erase female biological functions that she believed were the basis of male and female, and of inequality. Others felt that the answer was to end modes of gender expression, patterns of femininity and masculinity. Carolyn Heilbrun advocated androgyny, the elimination of the polarities of "gender roles" that she considered the cause of power differences between men and women. Andrea Dworkin campaigned to alter the practice of sexual intercourse, to get rid of sexual images and acts she believed would perpetuate maleness and femaleness, and therefore domination and submission.

I found these theories persuasive. Maybe eliminating sex differences or transcending gender expression would end *woman* as a place of oppression. But, in fact, the theories didn't explain some important aspects of oppression against me as a woman in my daily life. I'd been pregnant with two children and given birth to them. The way the doctors treated me only made me ask, "If there were artificial wombs, whose hands would administer the technology, and for whose profits?" And those two children had been two boys, each of whom had possessed, by the time he was two or three, his own unique blend of masculine and feminine. Was it possible to train them into androgyny? Was this the skill they needed to take action against unjust power in the world? As for intercourse, this was where I had experienced the most pleasure in my relationship with a man; my husband had tried carefully to please me. I would have had more pleasure if my sexual play had not been damaged by fear about pregnancy— and by shame about what I could want as a woman. But my husband's penis was not dominating my life. Instead, I was concerned about the power of white men who interviewed me for possible jobs at large institutions and then protected their economic position by never hiring me.

And, when I stood up to face the public opponents of my liberation as a woman, I got little help from the theories I was reading. When I debated right-wing women in my community in North Carolina, as they lambasted the Equal Rights Amendment, their tactics were based on baiting the women's rights movement precisely on the issue of elimination of sex and gender differences. They accused: Equal rights means unisex bathrooms. Equal rights means homosexual marriages. They meant: If you challenge gender boundaries, you will make women more vulnerable to abuse by eliminating gender protection. They meant: If you challenge gender boundaries, you will have men and women adopting the behavior of the opposite sex and getting pleasure from it.

I didn't know how to answer their raging remarks, accusations that were echoed throughout the United States as part of a concerted antifeminist campaign. Some of the first slogans I'd learned in the women's movement were "Biology is not destiny" and "Women are made, not born." I'd read feminist theory that analyzed how jobs and household chores and emotions were divided up between men and women according to sex. But I—and the primarily white middle-to-upper-class reform women's movement that backed the E.R.A.—did not have an analysis of sex, gender expression, and sexuality that was complex enough to respond to these right-wing attacks.

We could have said, in these debates, that the answer to violence against women was not the illusion of protection by limiting women's activity, but a movement in which women learned to fight back, with allies, to protect ourselves, and to move through the whole world safely. We could have answered that the split between *man* and *woman* was designed to keep one sex up and one sex down and in an economic system where profiteers make money off a war between the sexes. We could have answered that *woman* was not the opposite of *man*, and that liberation meant crossing all arbitrary gender boundaries, to place ourselves anywhere we chose on the continuum of maleness to femaleness, in any aspect of our lives.

In some more private spaces within women's liberation, we did advance these arguments. But in hostile public space it was controversial to propose even the slightest changes in "normal" male and female behaviors. *That* was to question the foundation of "civilization." The reform wing of the women's movement was proudly ambivalent about taking a stance on lesbian and transgender issues publicly. It dealt with issues of race and class reluctantly and inconsistently, when at all. A victory for these reformers meant only a fractional expansion of the old public boundaries on what was acceptable behavior for "womanhood," on who was a "respectable" woman.

Some of these reformists accepted limits on what constituted womanhood because of uncritical allegiances to their own class and race positions. For others, this was a strategic decision; they believed a political definition of woman that deemphasized difference would secure more territory for women in a hostile world. They hoped to establish a bulwark, and then a place that could be built on for greater liberation. In fact, the exclusion of women who blurred the edges of what was considered legitimate as *woman*—because of race or class or sexuality or gender presentation—made women's space smaller and more dangerous, made this aspect of the women's movement weaker and more limited in foundation.

In the end, I moved away from reform politics into cultural and political actions that embraced the complexities of *woman*. The group of women I began to work with was, at first, predominantly white, both working class and middle class, and lesbian. But we had been deeply influenced by the Black civil rights and liberation movements. We saw the freedom of all women as linked inextricably to the elimination of racism. In addition, we learned from the political and theoretical work of feminists and lesbians of color who showed us how to question—and place in an economic and historical context— the many categories of "difference," including those of race, sex, class, and sexuality.

But even as we traced how women's liberation could be extended through these connections, these untanglings and re-braidings, we still had not fully explored sex and gender. These were unanswered questions, and questions that were never raised, about "manhood" and "womanhood." We carried with us many of the negative assumptions and values that the larger culture had assigned to *woman, feminine, man, masculine*—ideas that served to limit women's behaviors and to prevent examination of how "masculinity" and "femininity" are not the basis of sex, race, and class oppression.

Often a lesbian considered "too butch" was assumed to be, at least in part, a male chauvinist. She might get thrown out of her lesbian collective for this, or refused admittance to a lesbian bar. Frequently a lesbian who was "too femme" was perceived as a woman who had not liberated her mind or her body. In ordinary arguments with a lesbian friend or lover, she could be dismissed—as I sometimes was—with, "You act just like a heterosexual woman." Yet during this same time, lesbians who were butch, femme, and all gender expressions in between were trying to decipher which of our behaviors still did reflect oppressive patterns learned in a woman-hating culture. These struggles were present in 1982, in New York City, when an alliance of women with a range of sexualities had planned "The Scholar and the Feminist" annual conference as a way to examine the complex intersections of pleasure and danger in women's sexuality and gender expression. They were condemned as "sexual deviants" and "sluts" by a group of women organizing against pornography, who identified themselves as "real feminists."

At about this time, I was teaching women's studies at a state university near Washington, D.C. One day in the classroom, we were discussing lesbian life in general, and butch/femme in particular. I was dressed casually, but in a femme style. The white woman to my left was a muscular, big woman, with short hair and a black leather jacket; she drove a Harley to school every day. She said forcefully, "Butch and femme don't exist anymore." It was a moment typical, in many ways, of the lesbian-feminist space I lived inside during the 1980s. As women and as lesbians we wanted to step outside traps set for us as people sexed as *women*, to evade negative values gendered to us. We didn't want to be women as defined by the larger culture, so we had to get rid of femininity. We didn't want to be oppressed by men, so we had to get rid of masculinity. And we wanted to end enforced desires, so we had to get rid of heterosexuality.

For some lesbians, one way out of these traps was to choose androgyny, or to practice a sexuality of "mutuality and equality"—an attempt to eliminate the variations of "man" and "woman" we saw in each other every day. Another way was to explain hostility toward "masculine" lesbians and "feminine" lesbians as arising from homophobia rather than from prejudices about what kind of gender expression was appropriate for "respectable" women and "liberated" women. One answer for many was to deny the deep fear in the larger culture, and therefore within ourselves, about sex and gender fluidity.

The fear can take different forms. The classified sections of gay and lesbian newspapers still run personal ads that say "No butches, no drugs"—a statement equating gender defiance in a woman with self-destruction, a lesbian version of a gay man's "straight-appearing, no femmes" ad. Discussion of sexuality may exclude butch/butch and femme/femme pairings as too homoerotically queer. Some of us who talk of ourselves as butch or femme may reject identification with people like us who live at the extremes of gender. A coolly sophisticated lesbian at a dance may say, "I'm a femme, but I'm not like *her*,"—dismissing the woman she sees as "going too far" in her femininity.

We know, from being alive in the United States in the twentieth century, that there are severe punishments dealt to those who cross sex and gender boundaries and terrible penalties visited on women who claim their womanhood independently. This is really no surprise, though, since the institutions of power are based, at least in part, on controlling difference—by sex, gender, and sexuality. No wonder we may feel there is safety in moderation, in assimilation, in a "normal" expression of sex and gender. But *moderation* means "to keep within bounds." Inside whose boundaries are we living?

And despite the punishments for boundary crossing, we continue to live, daily, with all our contradictory differences. Here I still stand, unmistakably "feminine" in style, and "womanly" in personal experience—and unacceptably "masculine" in political interests in my dedication to writing a poetry that stretches beyond the woman's domain of the home. Here I am, assigned a "female" sex on my birth certificate, but not considered womanly enough—because I am a lesbian—to retain custody of the children I delivered from my woman's body. As a white girl raised in a segregated culture, I was expected to be "ladylike"—sexually repressed but acquiescent to white men of my class—while other, darker women were damned as "promiscuous" so their bodies could be seized and exploited. I've worked outside the home for at least part of my living since I was a teenager—a fact deemed masculine by some. But my occupation now is that of teacher, work suitably feminine for a woman as long as I don't tell my students I'm a lesbian—a sexuality thought too aggressive and "masculine" to fit with my "femininity."

I am definitively lesbian to myself, but not in a way recognizable to a heterosexual world that assumes lesbians to be "mannish." Unless I announce myself to be lesbian, which I do often—in my classroom, at poetry readings, to curious taxi drivers—I am usually assumed to be straight. But unless I "butch up" my style, sometimes I am suspect inside my lesbian world as too feminine to be lesbian. And both inside and outside lesbian space, there is another assumption held by some. No "real" lesbian would be attracted to as much masculinity as I prefer in my lesbian lover.

How can I reconcile the contradictions of sex and gender, in my experience and my politics, in my body? We are all offered a chance to escape this puzzle at one time or another. We are offered the True or False correct answer. We are handed the questionnaire to fill out. But the boxes that we check, *M* or *F*, the categories *male* or *female*, do not contain the complexity of sex and gender for any of us.

The stories that follow are part of a new theory about that complexity which is appearing at the intersections: between the feminism of U.S. women's liberation; the writings of women of color nationally and internationally; the queer ideas of lesbian, gay, and bisexual liberation; the emerging thought of transgender liberation—a movement that embraces drag queens and kings, transsexuals, cross-dressers, he-shes and she-males, intersexed people, transgenderists, and people of ambiguous, androgynous, or contradictory sex and gender. These intersections make clear that every aspect of a person's gender expression and sex will not be consistently either masculine or feminine, man or woman. I find many layers of my own experience in this theory, and I find an exhilaration at the connections between myself and others as I see, with increasing clarity, how gender oppression and liberation affect everyone, how my struggles as a woman and a lesbian overlap and join with the struggles of other gender and sexually oppressed people. A friend of mine has said of this exhilaration: "It's like being released from a cage I didn't know I was in."

This is a theory that explores the infinities, the fluidities of sex and gender. The African-American woman eating sushi at the next table may be a woman lovely in her bones, gestures, tone of voice, but this does not mean that her genitals are female. If the handsome Filipino man in the upstairs apartment is straight-appearing, this does not mean his erotic preference is the "opposite sex." The white woman next to you at the doctor's office may have been born male and have a complex history of hormones and surgery. Or she may have been born female and have a different but equally complex history of hormones and surgery. The person on the subway who you perceive as a white man in a business suit may have been born female, may consider herself a butch lesbian, or may identify himself as a gay man. The *M* and the *F* on the questionnaire are useless.

Now here I stand, far from where I was born, from the small segregated hospital in Alabama where a nurse checked *F* and *W* on my birth certificate. Far from my first tomboy girlfriend and the ways we played together, splashing barefoot in rainwater. Far from who I was as a wife and mother, almost twenty years ago, when I began to question the destiny I had been assigned as a woman. I have lived my life at the intersection of great waves of social change in the United States in the twentieth century: the Black civil rights and liberation movements, the women's liberation movement, the lesbian/ gay/bisexual liberation movement, the transgender liberation movement. The theories developed by each has complicated our questions about the categories of race, sex, gender, sexuality, and class. And these theories have advanced our ability to struggle against oppressions that are imposed and justified using these categories. But we cannot move theory into action unless we can find it in the eccentric and wandering ways of our daily life. I have written the stories that follow to give theory flesh and breath.

I.

"SHE
WAS
THE
BOLD
ONE
WHOSE
FOOT
I
FOLLOWED
..."

PINK DRESS

When we were eight, she was the bold one whose foot I followed, branch to branch, up the sweetgum tree, up into the purple-black spicy leaves. Or her bare feet, callused as boots at the end of the summer, would move confidently across the stobs of cedar posts in the corncrib, to disappear into the hayloft, treading out the dusty golden remnants of grass, while I stuck wedged and timid below, feet sliding on cedar as thick as metal, polished by years of jostling cows. Eventually she would look over the edge, disdainful but patient, to advise how to set my feet, my weight, to step up with her into the stifling, fragrant heat.

When we were sixteen, I sat in the bleachers and watched her on the gym floor, balancing on a wooden beam the width of a train track's steel rail, no warning whistle while she tensed her muscles and jumped. In the evening, getting ready to go out, she stood naked before the mirror, her brown breasts' weight beginning to pull at her ribs. She dabbed Canoe aftershave behind her ears and between her breasts. I watched her, with the sharp taste of limes in my mouth, and the acid smell etching the palms of my empty hands.

When I was twenty-four or -five or -six, after she was married, and I was married, I saw a photograph of her in a pink dress, her hair cropped close and kinky, with gold hoops in her ears. She stood smiling as she curled a tiny white dog under each arm. Her breasts had filled out, and they pushed against the bodice of her sheath dress. I knew her body still, when I saw her, and a sudden desire took me forward, a surge as if I could reach and touch her breasts.

After I had touched another woman, and yet another, my mouth browsing their soft sharp nipples, I began to dream of her. One night she was far from me, sprawled on a towel on the beach. As I walked closer through the sand, I could see her legs were spread open. I could taste her salt; the air was briny with her. But kneeling between her legs, my tongue about to part her wiry pubic hair, I saw with horror that she was sewn closed, her labia crisscrossed in blood by dark metal threads.

I found a photograph of us when we were three, in front of an old farmhouse. She smiles behind me, diffident in a dress, dark hair pulled back in a barrette, legs bare, feet sandaled. I'm moving ahead of her, a rubber doll-baby gripped in one hand. I am unsmiling in my sturdy jumpsuit—brow furrowed, about to do something important, hand out, weight forward.

But I wanted her to be the bold one. I watched her ahead, feet agile in the next difficult position. Some day she would turn back and touch me. My desire set her in amber memory where she reaches back for me, hand out, through the golden dust of light.

WOMEN'S DANCE

She is not the first woman I have danced with. In high school I had a friend, a girl who sometimes held my hand in the dark, who once or twice whirled me around our music practice room. At the senior prom, when the girls outnumbered the boys and I went with my best friend, she and I didn't dance. But this lanky, studious woman is the first grown-up woman, a married woman like me, venturing into sisterhood at a graduate student's apartment in North Carolina. Not yet the collective house at Laurel Avenue, or the one on Green Street, this scruffy duplex is crowded with women who consider themselves part of women's liberation. Every poster on the wall, every note on the refrigerator, is about women doing things together. I want to copy the roster of rotating housework tacked up in the kitchen to use at home with my husband. But I've also just written a review for the local feminist newsletter—on a book about androgyny—so now I feel like I belong here, at my first women's dance. And now she and I dance one dance. No sparks with her except the thrill of asking for that dance. No conversation, although I wonder about her work as a graduate student who teaches storefront classes on women's history; the university won't let her do it for credit. Tonight she is my partner for one song at a dance I've come to mostly to spite my husband, who worries when I do women-only things.

I'm also fighting with some of the women in my university department because I want to close the Women's Caucus social events to men. One of them says to me, "My husband will feel funny," and I say, "No offense to him, but women often go places without their husbands." I don't know how to articulate to her what I can see, an enticing vista, what it might be like to talk amongst ourselves without always having to answer the men or reassure them. What kind of new plots might we come up with? What kind of endings invented at a potluck of just us?

Dancing with a woman who doesn't seem especially interested in me, I glance around the room and see, pressed into a corner on the margins of the dance floor, half-lying under a coffee table, two women making out. One, in a boy's cap, nuzzles the other's neck. I am repulsed and attracted. I'm watching something taboo, something pornographic, a peep show. But my body tingles as if I've raised a foot or hand bent too long in one position and the nerves have come suddenly alive.

My husband asks me nothing when I get home. The next afternoon I walk through the garden and meet our new neighbors. He's an ex-truck driver minister who was thrown out of seminary for political reasons; he's marched in Washington; he's a poet and handsome, like my husband. Standing next to him, I get as hot as if kneeling with my hands in garden dirt, a heat that lasts until he asks me to do him a favor— type up his notes for his evening sermon. I spend the rest of the afternoon alone, saving seeds in the garden, morning glories, scarlet climbers, cockscomb, prince's feather. I bend over withered vines and crush desiccated herbs in my hands, basil, dill, thyme. I lift up my fingers to smell the pungent oils.

SISTER

All the way south to the conference in Florida I lean forward from the back seat to argue with her, the passenger in front. She sits reared back, stubborn, her poufed, bleached, lacquered hair stiff as a backbone. I am talking to her about women's oppression, male supremacy, sisterhood—my arguments based on a book I've just read. Her mouth purses in disapproval. She has the style of some girls in my high school, wears frilly Sunday-go-to-meeting clothes too feminine for the university where we teach. We both have our jobs because some of the other women graduate students organized and demanded that teaching assistantships be awarded by sex in proportion to male and female enrollment. Before that revolt, almost all the jobs had gone to men, supposedly because they had families to feed.

She has four children and no husband. She married out of poverty at fourteen and left her husband just a year or two ago, in her mid-twenties, my age. I have two children and a husband I married three months out of my teens. I wear my body as awkwardly as I do my clothes, the handmade dresses my mother still sends me, the jeans and cast-off shirts from my husband. I decided in my teens I would be *mind,* not *body;* I would not let my girl's body trap me. All that would be left of *girl* would be the five-year-old oval frame in my mother's house. My pouting mouth, blonde curls, trick of cutting eyes at someone—that girl would be left there forever.

We drive into a horizon of black thunderclouds and heat. I argue with the woman who could be me, pale white skin and a drawl, but hers from West Virginia. I am arguing with myself. She has no time for our departmental Women's Caucus, the sessions for which I arrange refreshments, sherry, cookies, cups, cream and sugar, the evenings on "Nineteenth-Century Images of American Motherhood" and "Janet Shaw, Eighteenth-Century Lady of Quality, West Indies to North Carolina." She has no time and no money. She is struggling to keep her children with her after a bitter legal battle with her husband over custody. She needs to finish her degree in three years and become a professional so she can support them. I think she will have trouble, dressing the way she does, too sexual, yet acting too tough, an iron will under a lace blouse. At the conference, I get into a fight at supper with the man who is her date. He orders cheesecake and then says to another woman at the table, "I bet we've already got great cheesecake at the table. Why don't you lift your skirt so we can see?" He bends down to try and look at her legs and chuckles. I argue with him until finally I refuse to sit with him and leave.

I have no job interviews scheduled at the conference, but when I return to school I find the department has given me two classes, "Shakespeare" and "The American Novel," to teach in summer school. In my journal I note with glee that I am "beginning to feel professional." I hardly see my companion from the car after our return. I hear she has complained to some men in the department that she rode all the way south and back with two women who "hated men."

That spring I go into a gray depression. I sleep too much. I drink too much. I go to a movie alone for the first time in my life, a cold air-conditioned afternoon watching a man's story about a woman who mutilates her genitals. I feel the blood on my hands as she scrapes her insides out.

I wish I were running away in a car with another woman, driving farther south into the heat, sweating inside the translucent blue voile dress I wore the summer before I married, the one that no longer fits me after two children. I might argue with her all the way, but I'm arguing with myself: *How to be a woman?* I don't want to be. They do not see my mind, they only see my body. I don't want to leave my body. I want to feel full and humid, thunderhead about to crack with lightning. I want to walk in danger by myself and survive, the way she holds her head up, clenches her teeth under blood-red lips, and dares anyone to stop her. I don't want anyone to think I am like her. When we meet in the hallway at work, I can barely look at her, and she also looks askance.

WHITE CAMELLIAS

Every other week there are four, sometimes five, of us who sit on the carpeted floor of the Quaker House; we have started a consciousness-raising group. We talk about conflicts with men at work, at home, about dividing housework, about whether we are taken seriously as thinkers. During the summer that we meet, I stop writing in my journal. Instead, after I get the children to bed, I tell the man I'm married to that I'm shutting myself in the back room to work on my dissertation. There I secretly read Harlequin romances about a spirited woman who is trapped by convention, trussed in corsets, hidden in the heart of a boxwood maze. I read about the man who forces his way through to be with her. The delicious moment when his arm encircles her, his hand begins to pull at her ribbons. The prolonged arousing negotiation until he proves that this is love.

By the fall, I have moved with my family to another town in North Carolina. I commute to the CR sessions, long drives in which I mull over our topics. One week's assignment is to write on "Why did I get married?" Now that the children are in school, in the daytime I close the study door to read and fantasize: *I am a proper young woman kidnapped from my schooner by an equally proper pirate who holds me captive in his cabin and slowly seduces me.* I masturbate. I have three, four, five orgasms and am terrified at how much I long for someone to possess me, at how ferociously I try to possess myself with my own hand. In my group I finally say the word *masturbate*—which I've never spoken out loud in my life—and find the other women think the word and the practice are perfectly ordinary. They argue that men expect to masturbate and do, and women don't. They urge me to feel less guilty about the time I take for myself every day. When I sit down to do my academic work, I can't think. My skin feels sunburned. My breasts ache and chafe inside my blouse. My thighs and cunt are hot as if I'd been laying naked in the sun, on parched grass behind a tall hedge. I begin to write, but only in my journal about my dreams: *A woman and I are sitting together, talking and looking at a book. Suddenly I thrust my hands to her genitals and push her down. I wake flushed, aroused with astonishing passion.*

One day I reread letters from my husband when he was courting me. He wants to get his hands on me, he writes: *But maybe I should rephrase…rape you.* He thinks we will have handsome children and tells me: *You can take care of them by yourself.* In our daily life together since we married, he has shared housework half-and-half, and childcare the same since the birth of the first baby. In our sex life, though we never talk of what we want, he has been a considerate lover, always careful to bring me to orgasm, especially because penetration alone in intercourse is never enough for me. Was this courting language his dream language? What did he fantasize? What does he want to possess as he carefully pushes inside me?

I organize another CR group in the town where I now live. One of the women, who says nothing during the sessions, speaks to me afterwards about poetry, about Russian women writers. My husband comes home from a party and tells me that he saw this woman furtively kissing another woman there. Then one night, in the last five minutes of a meeting, she talks about having been raped. I begin to dream about her: *I am sitting next to her. I lean over and kiss her on the mouth, an exquisite lingering kiss, and I orgasm.* I wake up and feel my thighs and clitoris trembling, and I know I came for her in my sleep. I am bewildered that I've dreamt of her after she spoke of her rape. Do I desire her because she spoke the secret out loud, because she broke through the barrier between us? Do I desire her because she made herself vulnerable, showed me her wounds, a beckon to me to hold and heal her? Do I care for her only as a guide to follow down a path to myself? I wander between word, dream, fantasy, desire, action, man, woman, woman, woman.

By the spring our group is no longer meeting. I see her at a party. She flirts with me, and I flirt back. At midnight, when I leave both her and my husband there, I find a mass of white camellias, snapped from a tall hedge by the driveway, scattered over the windshield of my car. I know they are her sign to me. I crumple the stiff leaves and silky petals in my hands. The flowers smell like dust. I drive home and put clean sheets on the double bed I share with my husband. Crying bitterly, I lie down alone, vertiginous, nauseated with desire. When I sleep, I dream: *I am running down an endless sandy road, the dirt as fine as face powder. I am running from my husband who wants to kill me, to put me in a box, to blow me up.* In the morning, after I take the children to school, I sit in the backyard, in a patch of sun between hedges not yet in flower. I began to write a poem about my dream. I hold to my words as a thread out of a maze.

POCKET WATCH

I go with her to my first gay bar, by the railroad tracks in Fayetteville. An old white bulldagger comes to our table and politely asks me to dance. I think to myself wildly, *But I have a lover. Doesn't it show?* After I smile a no-I'm-with-her-nod, I turn to that first lover to hiss, "What are the rules here?" And she lies to me, for neither the first nor last time: "There are none." Later she leads me onto the tiny dance floor to kiss me roughly in front of the other women, kisses more fierce than she gives me in private. She doesn't explain why the butch asked me to dance instead of her, whose bright blonde hair falls below her shoulders.

Her birthday present to me is a gold pocket watch engraved with my initials, like the one she wears on a silver chain hooked to the belt loop of her slinky grey men's trousers. She gives me shirts like hers, flashy polyester disco, one where cobras writhe on the back, silver, red, black. She brings me out—a married woman—and tries to teach me to be *gay* without ever using the word. I begin to wear green fatigue pants secondhand from Fort Bragg, and T-shirts that demand *Free Joann Little*. I don't wear the watch on a chain, but carry it in my pocket. I take it out to check the time when I'm teaching and to shock my students, who may or may not notice.

When I am with her, I have no idea what sex I am or what gender, whose body I have, or the meanings of my gestures.

One afternoon I spread her legs with my hands and her labia with my fingers and dart my tongue deep into her. Satiated, I coil around her and fall asleep. In my dream I feel something swell between my legs, heavy and hot. Waking with a start in the dim twilight, in the rank sheets, first I am lying on my husband, his penis engorged against my stomach. Then it is her penis that burrows and bumps against me. Then I shift and know: perhaps it is my own, writhing and dreadful between my legs.

BARBED WIRE

One afternoon, when I am the speaker on women's liberation at a branch library near the mall, I debate a local representative of the Eagle Forum, a right-wing women's auxiliary. She and I wrangle over constitutional interpretations until she throws out a line like a whip: "Equal rights for women will make homosexual marriages legal, and men and women will have to use unisex toilets." I pause, stunned, and look at the ten people in the audience, who look back at me for a response to this statement that accuses: Either you like women too much, so you're a lesbian, so what you want is legal sanction for perverted sex. Or you don't like women at all, so you want to be a man, so what you really want is his filthy penis. At some point her accusations merge, and I become a perverted lesbian who wants a penis like a man and filthy sex with other women. She uncoils her words through the room like strands of wire she will nail to a fence. I struggle through my answer. I say of course we are for women, divorce law reform, equal pay. I say of course there won't be gay marriages or shared bathrooms. I try to say that lesbians are women too. I make a boundary around womanhood only a few feet larger than hers.

Just beyond it my woman lover and I lie in bed together in a cheap motel room. We're on our way north to Philadelphia, to a National Organization for Women conference, a long drive up and shared expenses with another woman. My lover puts her fingers on my mouth to shush me because of the sleeper in the next bed. She twists her fingers between my thighs, into my pubic hair. What kind of a woman can I be outside of this hidden room? Barbed wire marks off space allowed for woman, for man. To touch the boundary is dangerous.

After the library meeting, I go with some of the audience to a restaurant. We have cherry pie and coffee. A white woman stockbroker complains about quotas, a white housewife says that smiling at her husband feels like slavery, two women make jokes about queers. Two Black women who work for the county say, "You'll have to start talking differently if you want us to participate." Later, a N.O.W. member reprimands me, says that I shouldn't push lesbianism on the audience. But a year before, she'd been upset that I was afraid to tell her I was a lesbian. She was offended someone else had told her. Of my reticence, she'd said abruptly, "Being afraid to tell is your problem, not mine." I have had other arguments with this woman. I want the organization to back a Black woman who is suing the county for race and sex discrimination. She doesn't want to support the woman; she thinks that it would endanger local grants for our program funding. She tries to jerk me back from crossing the boundary.

After another library meeting, a consciousness-raising on rape, some of us go out to a bar. One woman was raped by a male friend, two others by their fathers. We get loud, noisy, annoying. Three white men in suits walk past us. One stops, puts his hand on the shoulder of one of the women who'd been raped, and asks: "Solving the world's problems?" She says, "I don't know about that, but take your hand off me." I say, "We don't know you. We don't want to talk to you."

I put barbed wire up between me and the intrusive hand that fondles, that rips, that pats and then slaps. When I go out in public, I wrap my body in barbed wire. I unwind it at night to be with my lover while both of us drink to numb the pain that tracks across our arms, our breasts, our thighs. Sometimes she mocks me when she fights with me, her hand and voice mimicking mine. With bitter laughter, she calls me *queer*. I wonder what kind of woman I would be past these boundaries. Maybe someone naked in a silk robe, the contours of my body shifting as fluid as the fabric, skin flexible as silk. How much of a man would I be? How much of a woman? If I could slip off the robe of my gender, my sex, who would I lie down with, naked?

STEAM HEAT

We are sweating as much from her song as from the early summer heat in Atlanta, three hundred lesbians packed into an old movie theater, sweating and sighing over a short, stocky butch in a tuxedo, lip-synching to "Steam Heat." She is the opening act for the Red Dyke Theater, on the opening night of the Great Southeast Lesbian Conference, and no one is better than she is that night, except the tall red-headed femme who jumps onto the stage next, cracking a black bullwhip. I sit, a still-married woman, next to my first woman lover, watching how to be a lesbian.

The next day my lover complains of how I relate to her around other women: I introduce her too possessively, I exclude her in conversations, I decide my workshops without her, I'm affectionate at the wrong times. All weekend I worry miserably about how ten years of married heterosexual life has distorted my behavior as a woman. Only later do I wonder about the connection between her contradictory accusations and the amphetamines and marijuana in her bedside drawer. In the meantime, I'm often ashamed when she kisses me in front of others. Awkwardly, we try to talk about sex and agree that we don't have to "take turns," that whoever wants it should have it. She likes my touch, that's new for her, says *butch* and *femme* are about who won't be touched and who likes to be touched. We don't talk about her fear of touch as connected to her rape, about touch that is the fist of ownership, nor her fear of laughter on the street that sneaks up behind her man's walk and her woman's breasts. We agree that we both seem to be femme, and I lie beside her wishing I was as clear about sexuality, maleness, and femaleness as that femme with the whip seemed to be.

On Saturday we walk in sweltering heat from dyke home to dyke home in Little Five Points. We attend workshops on wide wooden porches, drinking iced tea while sweat slides down our faces like beads of water on the glasses in our hands. In the Lesbian Mother Workshop, worried about my boy children, I ask if women there have had custody fights. No one is willing to talk about that. One woman says she has given her boys up to their father. Stretched out in oak shade during a workshop on FBI infiltration of the women's movement, I look at how the women are dressed: mostly jeans and shorts and T-shirts, some boyishly short haircuts, a few discreet hoop earrings. Nothing very bright or feminine. Maybe this would be the safe way to dress as a woman on my own, without a man, no calling attention to myself as sexual prey. Maybe men would leave me alone and other lesbians would say hello. Curious to have to dress less "like a woman" to find the women like you. Is it dressing in someone else's idea? Is it a belief that a woman who loves women really just wants to be a man, and so surely she will dress like one? Still, a feminist friend who says she's a radical lesbian *and* a femme comes to the dance that night in a diaphanous silk blouse over a slinky dress. She releases her hair and it swirls in snaky whips down to her waist.

But this is not how I want to look when I get home to a husband outraged over the love notes he's found stuck in my feminist books. He says he's closing the joint bank account and opening his own since he's the one with a job, he supports the family. I flush all over, skin red-hot with shame. I feel like a cheat and forget that I know about women and the law, the way we are loose property that reverts to the lord of the manor, the crown, the U.S. government. I forget that I've done most of the childcare, cooking, cleaning, and laundry for the last year. I forget I've read Angela Davis and Shulamith Firestone. At the conference, I had gone to every socialist-feminist workshop, exhilarating debates led by the Dykes for the Second American Revolution, the same women as the Red Dykes who'd done drag. We had imagined a liberation movement that offered both gender freedom and the end of capitalism. We had talked about how the concept of "professionalism" encouraged lesbians to identify with the ruling hierarchy and how revolutionary violence—such as robbing banks to finance the struggle—wasn't smart unless you had enough firepower to keep from getting wiped out.

At home, arguing with my husband in the kitchen, I panic. I have almost no money of my own. I wheedle and plead with him to give me a few weeks, and I decide that one definition of a lesbian is a woman with a job. When he slams out of the house, I sit down in a red kitchen chair and wish I were back in the auditorium, sweating and waiting for the show to begin. I would sing along with hundreds of dykes: *I've been cheated / been mistreated / when will I be loved?* And the woman next to me would answer.

ROCK

At first glance she looks like a pile of rocks, a landslide. Then I see that her massive back and thighs are stone and that the blue trickle of spring water is wetness spreading between her legs. I can't see her face, turned away in shame, in despair. Every day I sit on my sofa and stare at her stone back, and command her to turn and face me. I first began to dream about her, the woman in this painting, after I saw it in an art exhibit at the town meeting we'd organized on women's issues. The artist told me she'd begun the picture after her wedding night.

At that meeting, the speakers talked about violence against women, "minority" women, women in literature, women in politics. The paintings stood on easels behind the audience—women embedded in sand, women turned into dead rock, one pale woman with her feet in the swamp, a madonna rising out of the muck. At the end of the day, our last speaker was late, so I hurriedly wrote a closing talk that ended with the lines from the poet Judy Grahn: "'For all the world we didn't know we held in common … / the common woman … will rise.'"

I quoted another poet; I did not quote myself, notes from my journal, my anger at women who did not want to be called *feminist* because it meant *lesbian.* No public comments about ecstatic sex with my woman lover, the way she sucks my breasts until I fall asleep exhausted, my clitoris hard as a diamond between my legs. The way I fight with her into desperation at the accusation I treat her like a man, when I don't know what she means. The way I grieve my children, whose father threatens to take them away because I said out loud to him that I was a lesbian. The way my youngest cries in his sleep for me because he has an earache, but I am not there. When he tells me this, I hear a voice hissing in my ear, *Where have you been?* I answer, *In hell.* The way my lover wakes up screaming from a nightmare as a man opens his knife to rape her. I did not tell the audience that my lover, and the woman who painted the pictures, and I who organized the conference, went to town one night to go dancing at a new bar but couldn't get in. The police were at the door taking the names of anyone who entered that queer place while a bunch of straight white men from the army base taunted us, the promise of rocks in their clenched fists.

I went home from the town meeting and dreamed about a woman who was heavy and unmoving as a boulder. A week later I bought the painting from the artist, hung it on my wall, and went on with organizing. In the next eighteen months there was: the questionnaire to gather statistics on wife-beating, the women's karate class, the community forum on rape, the grantwriting for a displaced homemakers program, the Women's Day vigil and party, the support work for a Black woman's affirmative action suit against the county, the battered women seminar, the sexism in education seminar, the formation of a women's political caucus to canvas precinct by precinct for the Equal Rights Amendment. I talked to one person about my husband's threats. My lawyer said to me, "You don't have a dog's chance in court. Your affair won't last. They never do under the circumstances. Are you bisexual?

Normalize your life. You'll have a better chance for the children. Be careful. Don't count on his decency. Don't talk to her over your phone. Who do you love the most?"

I sit in the blue armchair, back from watching the children recede to a speck in the sky, on their way to their father's new home in another state. The phone rings with a call about tomorrow's name change petition at the courthouse and a call from a lover who does not ask about my children. I look at the painting across the room, her rough stone back. I am a woman embedded in the sediment of a culture hardened to stone. *Lie quietly, virgin girl, white woman, faithful wife, mother of sons.* My hands shake as if torn from hammering blows, breaking out from the inside. I vow, "I will not show what this is doing to me, not to people who despise who I am." No one will see tears falling down my face. I drink a bottle of thin sweet wine and listen to a woman singing a vague promise, an endless waterfall, a rock that will wear away. I make myself hard as the back of she who turns her face away from me. Any stone thrown at me will shatter.

CORNFIELD

On this night of the full moon, I've come with my old friend to celebrate my getting older, my birthday. We've had supper at the Southern Grill, a diner at a crossroads that has nothing else but a gas station. The restaurant's slogan is *Love at First Bite*, the perfect setting for a lesbian gothic vampire movie. As we leave, four blue-haired ladies in a booth by the door are saying: "She lies in bed and mumbles ... Except now that it's getting toward the full moon, she'll be howling ... I don't know how she stands it, being alone with her in that big old house." The harvest moon is low and yellow over the cornfields as my friend and I drive deep into the dark country. I tell her of the nights I've wanted to howl, bereft of my body. Why did it take me so long to know what I desired? Fumes of alcohol in a claustrophobic house. I was a girl saturated with numbness. Outside was the only safe place to be. The only safe touch was that of red clay mud, cool and heavy to my feet. No other memories of my body.

The rustling fields rush past us. My friend says she always knew she loved the other girls, the way her body felt when they ran together in the mowed grass of some sports field, along the chalk lines. She has said a kind of farewell the night before she married when, instead of a wedding supper, she had played one last game with her women's softball team. Earlier this summer she'd called me, sounding happier than I'd ever heard her. She'd joined a women's team again. Standing in a dusty field, she'd gotten her first hit in twenty-five years—a single over third base. The energy flew up from the earth through her cunt, belly, shoulders, into the bat. The power of the hit, her arms lifting and winging her toward all the other women running in response to her.

The moon rises higher and whiter in the sky as I see us both as girls, running lonely down some paved blistering street or muddy path. We took out forbidden love for ourselves, for other girls, and shifted our desire to something else, a sport, a hobby, a story, an object, a sensation. We took our bright dangerous energy, the crescent horns, the blade, and hid it somewhere so safe we almost could not find it again. Where had I hidden myself? The sultry nights on my bed, a teenager reading romances, adventure stories, tales of escape. Perhaps I could find someone else there, or perhaps be found. On summer mornings, lying very still in bed, I closed my eyes and waited for someone to touch me. Hours dreaming of someone stern, determined, almost rough, who could break down the door into the intolerable white sunlight of my lonely room. Then I would be seen. Then I would be made translucent with desire.

II.

"HER FINGERTIPS LEFT BURNING CIRCLES ON MY BREAST ...."

ROSES

In the summer she comes to visit me, and I decorate my bedroom with jugs of roses, blowzy pink-and-yellow roses from the fence around the house I share with two of the four lesbians I know in town. I pick her up at the bus station and bring her to my room, where I burn candles and sandalwood incense, and we slide between my cool sheets. In the winter I drive across North Carolina to stay with her at the Charlotte Women's Center where she's a resident manager. We lie in bed next to the radiator, naked in the steam heat, and she says she plans to change her name to something warmer. She tells me a story about the mountains, how one morning when she drove to work it was so cold and early that the clouds froze in the bare tree branches, armfuls of snow roses. She's a writer who's been telling me stories since I met her at a state women's conference. She was the only woman there who spoke as an out lesbian.

She is a skinny, flat-chested, tough blonde butch who is also the mother of a boy child. She brings me roses when we go out on a date. Our evenings are nothing like my college blind dates, like the one with the Kappa Alpha frat man who reminded me that Robert E. Lee had been a KA too, and then silently handed me his whiskey bottle in a brown paper sack to hold while he drove. Nothing like my dates with the Theta Chi president who needed a sorority sweetheart in time for the homecoming parade, me in a red wool suit waving from the back of his convertible, a dozen red roses on my lap. On our evenings together, she and I talk politics and words, what is *lesbian,* what is *revolution.* She knows the Drastic Dykes, the women I expect to show up at meetings in black leather jackets and chains; instead they wear jeans and flannel shirts and hippie dresses. She writes for a local lesbian literary magazine, *Sinister Wisdom.* I think she knows more about being a dyke than I do. Is that because she's a butch? We don't talk about this, and we don't talk about masculinity. We just talk about ending oppression by men. Sometimes we talk about how we should both drink less, and then we do for a while.

When I drive down to see her, I wear a blouse open over a man's white undershirt. When I pay for my gas, the attendant points to a sixteen-wheeler in the lot and asks, "Is that your truck?" If he's joking, I don't care. Maybe I can drive into a third space that is *lesbian,* and not *woman* or *man.* I'm ready to live outside of femaleness, the hedge of roses, thorny and beautiful, that has encircled me wherever I've sat waiting. Once, when I tried to write my way out, the poets who were men said to me, "Beauty is its own excuse for being." Now I make poems for her where her vulva petals turn into blade-sharp teeth. I caress the edge of her sex with my tongue. But one evening after we've made love, after we've both been drinking too much, she says to me, "You're so good at this you could sell it." I am speechless with rage. I have no way to reply: *Roses are sold on the street. Are bruised petals, furious thorns, the same as paper money crumpled in the hands of the seller?*

FIST

She pushes her fingers into my mouth as we lie side by side on the bed, and I begin to suck. I want her whole hand inside my mouth, like a hand in my cunt, but a different type of fisting. With each finger, she teases my tongue as if it were fingering my clit. All of my consciousness is on the tip of my tongue where her forefinger touches. I eat her hand, trying to get more and more of it deep into my mouth. How much can I take without gagging? I want her hand to reach down into my stomach and grab. Wring out some painful emotion—not love, but something close. My mouth fills with this, a kind of sex I haven't understood. Delicately I bite each of her fingers and the flesh webbed between. I could clench my jaw and break each slender bone. My tongue rests on her palm. The grooved lines there may mean long life or broken hearts. I don't try to read the enigmatic script as I take her hand down to where I devour everything.

CLOSED DOOR

She says, laughing, that she's lectured students for years about the oppression implicit in the gesture of door-opening, the way that men's mannerly care vanishes when women really need to be helped with a burden. Now, my new affair says, she finds herself with an impulse to door-opening. She doesn't elaborate, but I know she is thinking about me, how she drove me home one night from dinner and kept her right hand on me while she steered and shifted with her left. I held her hand in mine, blissful to be handled after years of no touch. When we got into the car, did she open my door for me? Perhaps she did that night because she had the keys in her hand. I say to her, "What will you do the next time you are confronted with me and a closed door?" She answers lightly but seriously, "If your arms are full of packages, of course I'll open it for you." I don't want another answer, but I don't quite believe this one.

I imagine us walking into a bookstore, deep in flirtation, and I see her, smiling, reach past me to pull open the door. In this fantasy, she is not like a man who ostentatiously opens a battle of wills over who controls going in and coming out. And she certainly does not resemble a man who reaches out to repeat, by habit, a gesture of his strength, my weakness. She has said to me, "A butch is not a man." Now I say, "A femme is not a woman, at least not the woman people think.

It's a case of mistaken identity." The opening of the door between us is not about whose power limits the other. I smile at her, invite her to advance down some vista with me. She smiles back, agrees, takes my arm, says, "Shall we?" and opens the door. Sometimes I pull her through when she hesitates, a sudden panic about the terrors of the opening body.

For a few months she sends me cards, one after the other, views through a framed, arched, buttressed, open door. I keep looking, but every time, what I see through the archway is that she stands in a green enclosed garden with another woman, her other lover.

MAMA

When she comes for a visit, after I've moved to D.C., my dyke neighbors ask us over for dessert. I attend to how she gets through a social situation I'm sure she's never faced, an evening at home with an African-American butch and an Iraqi femme. As we four lean toward each other over hazelnut coffee, I wonder if she's ever sat down to eat in an interracial group. But my friends are interested in something else: "We expected a little white lady in gloves. You didn't tell us that your mama's a bulldagger!"

She has been the woman who sat at the grey kitchen table with my father, her child and her husband. She was always the one next to the stove, within reach of the pot of field peas, more cornbread. I'm so used to this that I saw her hands simply as feminine, though they are huge, capable with iron mattock or steel knitting needles. I'm used to her height and bulk, her sneakers and windbreaker, her taciturnity and her ease with women, that I've never noticed how much she looks like the white-headed coach of a women's softball team.

But when we go to an all-woman, all-lesbian, New Year's Eve party, I pay more attention. Mama, heated with wine, in a purple sweatshirt, in a mask of extravagant feather, fast-dances and flirts with a red-headed merry femme, and then with another woman, nimble in cowboy boots. When I ask her which women she liked, she says, simply, "They're the ones who asked me to dance." The next afternoon, at the New Year's Dance reception, she is stiff, self-conscious, as women mill around her. Afterwards, she reminds me that she is always shy in crowds; and I see how she would lean awkwardly against the corner of a bar, watching the women play pool, maybe a glass in her hands to give them something to do. Later in the week, as we cruise the shopping malls, she exclaims over the beauty of the women who saunter past, but only the ones who are small energetic brunettes. She says they remind her of the woman she goes to basketball games with, whose forceful driving she much admires. Of this woman daring the other cars to hit them as they crash out of the stadium lot, Mama says with mock horror, "I just sit next to her and watch!"

In an old picture she is a skinny young brunette, hair pulled back with barrettes, shoulders stiff in a print dress, standing beside my father. She says of herself as a bride: "I was so little then, he could put his hands around my waist and they would meet." In that moment she looks femme to his butch, but in another photograph, walking in wartime downtown Birmingham next to a woman friend, she strides masculine and severe in a skirt suit. In her picture as a young bride, she does not touch my father; he has a cigarette in one hand, the other hangs loosely. The absence of touch in our house. What did she want that she could never get from him, or give, a sensation that she never let herself imagine? Whose softness under her hand? Or her strong back yielding under someone's weight, beneath her cheek? I lived in the house of her deprivation.

As we walk between stores still glittering with the fake opulence of the holidays, as we settle into a table at the food-court with ten international Americanized cuisines, I develop a half-serious theory to explain our years of difficult interactions: Maybe a butch mama usually raises a femme daughter, but they can't be buddies. Nor can they flirt, especially if the daughter is a tall blonde and the mama prefers petite brunettes. And so they stumble awkwardly with each other, as we have done, never knowing where to put their hands when they stand near each other.

In the souvenir photo of Mama and me on a New Orleans riverboat for her eightieth birthday expedition, she is big, tall, square to the camera, muffled in her jacket, feet spread wide and planted, both huge hands firmly grasping the rail, dark glasses another mask for her self-containment. I have twined both of my arms around one of hers, am leaning into her, head tilted, body tilted, dangling earrings, long coat, scarf, smiling for both of us. My butch mama—who I have tried to please, my hand on her forearm, femme insistence that we *know* each other. My butch mama—who has sat next to me at her kitchen table and told me, shivering, how much it disgusts her that I am a lesbian.

GREEN SCARF

Christmas morning I'm in a cotton undershirt and panties, straddling the floor grille of the gas furnace, a gush of warm air up around my thighs and cunt. Dangling from my hands is a green scarf, a present from my mother. I giggle and thread it between my breasts, around my bare shoulders, perhaps between my legs. My lover of six months sits watching on the edge of my tousled bed. I walk towards her, playing at being one of the ships that come sailing in on Christmas day in the morning. I make the scarf billow and puff, silky cloth about to carry us towards reefs, shoals, the narrow opening between rocks, the way to safe harbor. I advance towards her, my breasts dangerous and innocent. She says, "Stop it." She looks away, repulsed. Then she says I remind her of a girl she wanted in high school—blonde, heterosexual, femme. She doesn't say if she ever touched the girl. She says, "Don't act like that." I sit down on the bed; she puts her arms around me. The creamy warmth that flowed as I walked towards her congeals and stiffens in the crotch of my panties.

In the spring we go out to supper. She parks the car beside a restaurant, and damp air flows with blue neon shadows through the open window, over my face, into the curve of my neck, the dip between my breasts. I am languorous, as if swimming underwater in the dim light of the depths. When I surface, smiling, towards her familiar face, ready to come out into public with her, she leans over and fastens the top button of my blouse. A wave of shame stings my skin. I ask, "Why did you do that?" She says, "I didn't want anyone else to see you exposed." The tips of her fingers leave small burning circles on my right breast, like the imprint of a lit cigarette ground out in beach sand.

In the summer I come to her door with hair freshly cut, shorn short as a boy's, but with soft tendrils around my ears and neck. With hair this short, in jeans and T-shirt, I've been called "Sir" once or twice by those who easily ignored my breasts. Maybe now I look like a young sailor on shore leave, maybe now I look like an adventure. When I step into her hallway, she stares and says, "You've cut it so short. Now people will think you're the butch." She turns away without touching me at all, leaving me motionless in the cool passageway.

VERA

I go to the hospital every day to rub her feet with rose oil and lavender salve. Her big feet, size twelve at least, loom in my hands, with pale soles and arches, darker instep and ankle. Her skin, dry from months of chemotherapy, crumbles under my touch like dead leaves. She is sore everywhere. The wound in her belly is blood-rose red against her dark skin. I rub her back, which hurts all the time. I rub her feet until my hands can recreate every crease, every line of flesh that has borne her stone weight and presence through a short lifetime of hard work.

Towards the end I can do nothing but rub her feet. Sometimes we talk about how much has changed in our lives since we met, what we've learned together about our families and whiskey and pain. We've learned to get through the pain of the day, hers and mine, a minute at a time. Sometimes I listen as she tells me about being alone in the labor room of the hospital in Florida, fourteen years old, and the white doctor who slammed his fist into her face because she was screaming with pain, how she went home with a baby boy and a black eye. She tells me about sitting in the Job Corps dorm in Oklahoma as the trainees from New York City came off the bus, her eyes lighting on the femmes and the butches flaunting their style. Later, on the way to her first date with a woman, she remembered them, bought a painter's cap, put on

69

jeans and an Oxford shirt, rolled up her sleeves, and stuck her Luckies in. She'd watched the other dykes. She knew better than to carry on her date the purse that she took to her day job at the garment factory.

She tells me about trying to take care of her woman and her son, the construction jobs she worked as the only woman, the only African-American woman at every site. The bosses told her she did her work better than any of the men. She built prefab trailers, and she insulated houses, going up into attics in the summer to spray asbestos in suffocating heat, no protection from the glassy dust finer than pollen except a flimsy facemask. We both know the work she had to do to feed herself and her family had ended up killing her, but what else could she have done?

One day, on morphine, she tells me how she fantasizes escape from the hospital to go shopping. "What would you buy?" I ask, and she says, grinning lasciviously, "The first thing I'd get—something sexy for my baby—a black see-through lace nightgown." And for herself, "Some purple Birkenstock sandals, very comfortable for my feet." In her closet she has a pair of red leather hightop Nikes sent to her by her dyke sister for the day she walks out of her sterile, isolated room. Meanwhile, in its cool dark, we pretend we're strolling through the mall into a Cineplex Odeon. I go past the nurses' station down the hall and heat popcorn in the microwave. We eat it and watch an old movie about Josephine Baker on the rented TV.

The day before she dies, I bathe her all over, her big strong body shrunken in on itself but still beautiful in shades of darkness and rose. With water I freshen her face, her neck, her wide shoulders and strong arms, the aureoles of her nipples, her tender labia, the crease of her ass, the pink and brown creases of her feet. I complete the ritual of washing with not much soap, a little bit of skin with the rest covered by sheet, then rise, pat dry, then another leaf of skin revealed, then the painful lifting and heaving to get to her back, to change her diaper, the special soap to guard against bedsores, the ointment of vaseline and cornstarch. Last I wash and dry her feet and sit at the end of the bed with them in my hands, rubbing in the sweet salve. I sit holding her feet and tell her again I love her. And she says once again that she loves me before I leave.

The next morning, when I come with her lover to stand by her cold and stiffening body, she is already encased in her plastic coffin bag. I can only rest my hand on the outline of her toes. Later at their apartment, her lover pulls clothes out of the closet to send home to Florida with her body. She says, "We talked about the funeral, and she wanted her good black pants, and this purple Oxford shirt. I'm not sending anything else down to them. She made me promise not to let them bury her in a dress. I'll send only those clothes with her black penny loafers she kept shined up so nice." In my hands the shoes are brittle and empty as broken husks, as shed skin, their only liveliness the bright pennies that still wink in their sockets, as we refuse to weigh her eyelids down in final oblivion.

III.

"YOU SENT A BLACK-AND-WHITE POSTCARD, AN AMBIGUOUS FIGURE ... ."

THE OLD DAYS

Standing in the pit of the auditorium, you are someone I don't know yet, handsome in a silky shirt and tie, hair clipped close almost as skin on your fine-boned head. You read a story about bar raids in the '50s, a dawn scene on the street between a butch just released from jail and the woman who has waited for her, who now smooths her shirt and mourns the bloodstains that will never wash out. As you read, I am the woman who touches the shirt, startled to be so translated to a place I think I've never been.

Yet later I remember that when I got to the trailer she had already showered and changed out of her overalls. The plaid shirt, her favorite shirt he had slashed with his knife, was a heap on the bathroom floor. I thought then that he had raped her because she was a lesbian. But he raped her because she was also a butch, her cropped hair, her walk, three o'clock in the afternoon, taking out the garbage to the dumpster behind the 7-Eleven, finishing up her shift. I smoothed her shirt over my knees. I pinned the frayed plaid together. I hand-sewed with exquisite care until the colors matched again, trying to keep us together.

In the dim light of the auditorium, you see me standing in your past. Your message on my phone machine the next morning says, "So glad to see a femme from the old days." I write to you, to explain about my lesbian-feminist political coming-out. In return, your letter says, of me listening in the auditorium, "While I was reading, it was as if you were moving emotionally with me in the symmetry of a slow dance." I don't understand what you mean, me who begins to wander off in my own direction halfway through every dance with a lover, my attention and my confidence failing. I reply, dubiously, hopefully, "I have so much trouble following—perhaps I haven't had a skillful enough partner?"

When you come to visit me in D.C., we go to dance at the Phase. You have a pocketful of quarters and arrange for three slow Anita Bakers in a row. I am nervous and tentative for the first song and a half; you murmur endearments and instructions. Then suddenly I lean back in your arms, look into your eyes, and begin to move as if the dance is air I am flying into, or water I am finning through, finally moving in my element. When we sit to drink Calistogas and lime with friends, you say, "I never thought I'd dance again with a femme lover in a bar like this, like the ones I came out into." Behind us the jukebox glows like a neon dream, and dykes at the green baize table are clunking their pool cues. I tell you about my first bar, in North Carolina, almost ten years after the Stonewall Rebellion in New York City, an uprising of lesbian and gay liberation that I had not yet heard of. At that bar we parked around the corner so the police wouldn't photograph our license plates. We had to sign a roster at the door because it was a "private club." Rumor was that the lists got handed over to the police. My friends taught me to give a fake name; sometimes I signed in as Susan B. Anthony. Everyone always turned around to see who was coming in when the door opened. Everyone knew about the second exit in the dance room, double doors onto the street just in case of a raid, which never came while I was there. You lean towards me, tie loosened, shirt sleeves rolled up in the heat. You pull me into the hard circle of your arm and say, "Baby, no one knows about the second exit except someone from the old days."

DRAG BAR

You wonder what I was doing those years between your past and our present. Was I married? Was I single in the bars while I turned around to look for the butchest woman there? The summer before I met you I was sitting at a round, unbalanced table at the Bachelor's Mill, waiting for the show to begin.

I stirred a nonalcoholic tonic and lime while my date for the evening drank scotch. She was cool and handsome in a white linen jacket, just a friend, but her feet were seductive in cowboy half boots. I could see a bit of her white-socked ankle between shoe and trouser leg. I wondered briefly about the texture of her skin, taut over the ankle bone. Another couple sat across the dance floor, not quite our mirror image, brown to the white of us. One, a woman in a yellow dress, had haggard circles under her eyes and a little clutch purse. We circumspectly debated the sex of the person next to her: Unsmiling. Slender in all-black, in shirt and tie, men's suit, men's socks and shoes. Collar-length wavy hair brushed severely back from her face. Silent, head inclined to listen to companions, adjusting shirt cuffs once in a while. I kept looking directly across, let my eyes glide casually from the dancers to the watcher, my eyes lingering over the elegant hands, the somber mouth. Twice, three times, without moving in any other way, she let her eyes drift toward me, an almost invisible movement, delicate as breath exhaled on my cheek by a stranger leaning across me on a crowded dance floor. As her cool gaze touched my hot one, I tremored between my legs. Cool fingers on the hot pulse of my clit. My cunt clenched, an effort to have her, instantly. For only a second—then I tactfully shifted my angle of vision to the left, then back to a dancer off in my own direction halfway through every dancer.

Her look slid off me at almost the same moment.

She was the first person to stand up and slowly walk across the stage when the performances began. She folded a dollar bill into the sequined cleavage of a lip-synching drag queen, stately and bronze. She strolled almost as if not about what to do what she did, that intimate gesture. She didn't touch any of the women who were also dancing that night, nor call their sweaty half-naked bodies over to her. My date asked, "What do you think? Is she a butch?" And didn't listen as I said, "Yes, of course she is. She looked at me." Instead, my friend whispered to me, "I aspire to that style," and gave me a little lecture on *butch* as the achievement of perfectly mono-chromatic clothes. I did not answer. I was thinking that finally I understood the stories: How a single long look by a butch at someone else's femme once caused fistfights over that split second of possession. I did not say that if she had looked longer, and inclined her head toward the back room, I would have gone.

What was I doing all of those years? Waiting for you to look at me, just once.

CAMISOLE

We sit on the floor, your back against the couch and me between your legs, my ass resting against your trousered thighs. You say, "Take off this pretty thing," lifting one strap of my lace camisole. You ask if I'm cold as you rub my shoulders and arms with lavender oil. You breathe harder, the pulse of your chest light against my naked back. Your starched shirt rasps my skin, friction of thin cotton. Your breath quickens as you bend to bear me away. Your left arm curves across my shoulder and throat. My face flushes, almost a hot flash, the shadow of an old bush. I let myself lean back. You take the edge of my ear in your warm mouth. I lift your hand and lick each finger, and the webbing in between, and wonder when to mention safe sex. I say, "We'll be more comfortable on the couch." I get up, light a candle, turn off the lamp. When we lie down, you put me on the inside, you enclose me. I begin to melt into the curved mold of your body's length. Your silver belt buckle presses cold against my belly. I lift my head and say, "If we are going to go on, we need to talk about how to do this safely." You do not look surprised; later you tell me no other date has ever asked. On this first night I don't want to know your history. I tell you I want to take care of myself as if we are at the greatest risk.

I play no guessing games; I do not hide myself from you coyly. I am lying half on top of you. Your skin smells like smoldering sage leaves. My skin begins to blaze and I uncover myself. I am a woman turning her past inside out. I am a woman without shame. In the warm shadows I calmly talk to you, almost a stranger, about what I want. Later, after finger cots and latex gloves, and saran wrap with lubricant underneath, and a dildo harnessed with its condom, you say to me, "I'll give you anything you want in bed. It's the only place in the world where I can do that, and I will."

In the morning I sit naked on the couch, sunlight hot on my back, the camisole crumpled on the floor. I think: *If I can ask for touch, I can ask myself to do anything I want.*

BOOTS

The second time you and I met, we talked in a crowded room, and I hesitated when we said hello, my hands briefly on your arm, my mouth slightly flicking your cool thin lips. After we said goodbye, I saw you walk by and look at me out of the corner of your eye, a wild startled look, like that of an untamed horse. I wanted to take you by the hand and lead you to me: *Drink at my body, say you can't stop kissing me.* In your letter you said that you were hardly ever touched. It made you feel human to have a woman, a femme, put her hand on your arm for even a second. I was afraid to touch you, to become animal, sexual creature, the woman who wanted to be touched in return.

Now I walk to where you wait in my backyard, lying stretched out on the picnic table under the crabapple tree. Hands under your head, completely at home, you stare into the tree and the depths of the sky. You are waiting for me, and that is the power I walk in as I come down the back steps through the honey scent and white foam of autumn-flowering clematis. I sit beside you on the table, and you turn toward me. You curve your body so I am in the clasp of your hip and thigh. Why do we start talking about danger? I say that sex is the most physical risk I have ever taken, the femme equivalent of white water rafting. You laugh. You ask, "Nothing else?" I add, "Riding horses," and you want to know what I liked about that. "Making an enormous animal do what I wanted, the most precise motions, just by squeezing my thighs." You tease, "I bet you could do that with butches too." I arch my neck and say, "*Some* of them." One rainy afternoon at the sulky races, the winning driver snapped his long whip in the air and the bay horse leaped in response. The flick of sex in my clit, the shame at craving that moment.

Later we come home from the bar, where you made me yours with your hand unrelenting on the small of my back, where I worked my hips against yours. You lie on the bed, sweating, and reach for me. I say, "No." I kneel between your legs and slowly, one at a time, pull your black boots off. I kneel over you, my black silk skirt spread over your hips. I unbuckle your belt, unfasten your tie, unbutton your shirt, slowly slide away everything that guards and hides you. I say, "You are beautiful." I tell you, "Wait." I turn you over and sit, my thighs pressing against your naked hips, my cunt wet on your ass. My hand drifts lightly down your back as I feel you begin to leap and gather under me.

MARKS

She took my foot in her lap and circled my ankle with a bit of slender twisted leather, an anklet like girls wore when I was in high school, except this one was a souvenir from a woman's music festival. Sliding her fingers lightly over the skin of my ankle bone, she spoke of her distaste for permanent marks. She said, "I don't wish to do anything with you that is a mark of possession." I described to her the tattoo I wanted, perhaps a snake writhing from my wrist up my arm, perhaps a blue geometric bracelet. I argued with her about marks.

I said that we make them—alphabets or tattoos—as a human act to place the self in time, in location. If my beloved agrees to my teeth on her neck, then the tiny bruise is like a poem written to join the self passionately to another. The mark only becomes a trap when we begin to use it to save ourselves, when the wedding ring becomes a gold coin to buy security, eternity. Then we fix the other with an X: mark the spot, stay the same, be mine forever. We become unable to possess and then relinquish.

In this long, abstract conversation, neither of us said we were talking about sex. I did not speak of my need to be completely taken by a lover, how I wanted the fiery print of her hands everywhere on me, inside and out. Later, after she'd returned to her home, she sent me a packet of peel-on, wash-off tattoos, roses with thorns, salamanders, little dragons breathing fire.

You are lying on top of me, at the end of our first week together, and we are playing at being sixteen, having forbidden sex. I feel the edge of your teeth as you kiss my neck roughly, as you cry out, "I want to mark you, I want to." I am panting, "Go ahead, bite me, bite me." With my hand I pull your head toward me. You groan, "I *want* to, but I can't. I can't. I want to." I taunt you, I urge you on. You know I am going to another soon, but only I know there will be time for the marks to fade. I say, "Mark me," and you bend to my neck in possession against your principles. You lie on me again and say, "I don't want her to touch you. I don't want her to have your mouth, my god, to have your mouth." I lie quietly under you, I listen, I say nothing. But silently I admit to myself that I want this from you, to be claimed by you. The next day you say, "I want to possess you, not own you."

Later, over the phone, back in your city far away, you tell me, "When I first kissed you, I felt how you protected your heart." You say, "I'm coming back to kiss you again. You will open your mouth to me and I will touch your heart with my tongue." The invisible mark your lips, teeth, tongue will leave on me. By the time we have this conversation the marks on my neck, the bruises, are fading. I have called my other lover to tell her I am never coming to bed again.

SUGAR TIT

You say, "I've wondered how you'd explain what it's like to be lovers with someone seen as woman and man." I think of the dance we went to at a friend's house, the whisper about you repeated to me, "Well it must be a woman, it's with you. But she's wearing men's pants and men's shoes." I don't point out to the listener that I am the only woman at the party wearing a skirt. Of the other women, all with short hair and jeans and slacks, some are femmes, some butches with their legs spread apart and their hands in their pockets, some are kiki or androgynous. But no one pushes masculine and feminine to the edge of women as we do.

We slow-dance, even to the fast songs. Every so often, the same woman, drunk, walks by and says loudly, "They're still doing it. Did you only learn one step at Arthur Murray's?" Whispers sidelong glances from a group of younger white dykes. We decide to keep dancing; we don't know what else to do. An older crowd arrives, more African-American women. A femme friend comes over to laugh and joke. When you fast-dance with her, the same drunken woman says, "You *can* do that—why didn't you?" And you reply, "But this friend isn't the woman I love." I move with you and against you, slipping back and forth, shifting the earth under our feet.

Later you say to me, "You gave me everything in front of them." How they stared as you pulled me to you, hand on the small of my back as we danced, your thigh between mine, grinding gently. Your grip on me inexorable and sure, my counterpoint crossing you with my hips. How you began to sweat with desire, and the effort of working against my desire, your arms and legs the channel I flowed between, surging like a river released from underground. You held me as we danced, your shirt wringing wet, and the other women stared at us sliding in and out of womanhood. My skirt swung up around my hips. The last man I'd danced with was my husband, whose hands longed for me to hold him like a mother. The last woman I'd danced with wanted me to follow, but her hands weren't strong enough to hold me. You know that when you hold me, I will follow. You know I will give you my breast, but not as sugar tit. You long to see how much pleasure I will let flow through my nipples like milk, gushing and falling on the ground, perhaps in your mouth, perhaps on my own hands for me to lick off.

BEARD

In the grainy black-and-white video, a young dyke with a face smooth as an eggshell smears lather on her cheeks and neck, draws a razor across her face and throat. She talks to the audience: "I asked a girl to marry me, and she said, 'Girls can't get married to each other.'" The actress strokes away her imaginary beard with another flourish of the blade, and adds, "So I waited to become a man. I got tired of waiting. Waiting gets tiresome."

When you turn your face to kiss me at a certain angle, I am caressed by an edge of roughness, a rasp of hair at your chin's edge, a reminder of why on the street you're sometimes still taken for a man, an edge that reminds me how you lived as one. If you were bearded when we met, would I have let you kiss me? Would you have told me you were a woman? Or a man? What would you have said of who you were? Would the rough hair on your face have brushed against my mouth, made me want to part the soft hair curled between your legs, made my hands ready to caress whatever edge of flesh I found there?

ASHES

You told me you began to cry when you read the word *ashes* in one of my poems. You didn't know why. Sitting in this barren hotel room, I dial *2* over and over on the phone to hear my voicemail, your message left at 10 p.m. At the end, your voice breaks again and again on the first syllable: "Baby, baby, do you still love me?" Lonely here, with the loneliness of years, I am reassured by that one faltering tone. The voice of the stone breaking open to the streak of crystal. Your sun-hot streak against the papery skin of the palm. I have the power to break apart the rock. Fire inside. Wanting you to take me, burn me up, nothing left of me but ashes, potash to the ground. Wanting you to sift me through your hands, disperse me, gather me up again, handle me, your hands gritty with me, as all the while you call me "Treasure. Precious."

PA

On my way to supper with a friend, to gossip about love affairs, mine and hers, I put the photographs of you in my bag, the black-and-white ones taken in San Francisco. You squat in the front of a graffiti wall in your gray suit, elegant nonchalance against the dirt. You stand in the dappled sunshine and the weeds with your jacket slung over your shoulder like a film noir movie star. I gloat over the pictures and then pause to clear a few more pieces of debris from my desk. I sift through the mess of papers, turning up another photograph, my father and mother soon after they were married. She stands like a schoolgirl, feet primly together, hands behind her back, but this time the one I see is my father. They are side by side, but he does not touch her. His eyes are cautious under his fedora. In his double-breasted suit, cigarette in hand, he is a man of the world, debonair. I meet his eyes, and my heart shuts and opens under my breastbone as if you had come up behind me and slid your hands around my waist.

The last time he touched me without thinking first, he held my hand. I was three or four, and I was his. He tipped his Panama hat to everyone he met as they admired his baby, too young to be a girl, who twirled on the lunch counter stool while his buddies fed her ice cream. He carried her across the shining river on his back. On the muddy bank he yelled, "Hold 'em," as she jerked spiny invisible catfish out with a cane pole. He said, "Jump like me, run like me," and when she couldn't, he walked away. Her mama said to a neighbor, "He did want a boy." In his rocking chair, he watched Friday night boxing, Saturday afternoon baseball. He watched the boys he had once been write their names in the air with fists and arms. He rocked, he drank beer, whiskey, moonshine, he rocked and cried. At the funeral home, his best friend sat in her white Oxford shirt and her brown polyester slacks. She sat with her knees spread wide apart and chain-smoked Camels, like him. She told the story of how, many years ago, he would not go to see the brother he loved most in the world be married. She pressed two fingers tight together. "He loved him like this, like this," she said, her fingers lying close together as lovers.

The second time I met you, I wondered if we would be lovers. In a theatrical foyer crowded with dressed-up lesbians, you were wearing your gray suit. You were armored, aloof. I wanted to put my hand on your arm, but I thought you were saying, "No." Yet later, by myself in the night, I closed my eyes and returned to you, wordlessly, and without a word you gathered me into your arms. You sent a black-and-white post-card, an ambiguous figure in a trenchcoat, pants, heavy shoes, striding through the steam of a manhole cover, rising up from the underground. If I had sent you a photograph of myself then, it would have been the white flowers of jimsonweed, almost angel trumpets open at dusk in a waste place, against the cement rubble of a city block, or on limestone rocks jumbled by the river.

You told me, over and over, that you wanted me to be your girl. Now sometimes you call me your femme, or you say, "You are *so* smart, that's why I call you *girl*." Sometimes I hold you, brushing my hand over the silky stubble of your hair, and say, "You're my girl, you're my boy." Now when we lie together you hold me and infinitesimally rock me, rock me, caught in the backwash of the river. Not my mama nor my pa ever rocked me this way, timeless, the little waves lapping at the muddy bank, leaving a thin script, a tender mark on the skin of dirt.

MARRIAGE PROPOSAL

I say to myself: "I married the first time so I could have sex. I don't have to marry to have sex." The man I married taught me, just before we married, what an orgasm was. He showed me how his hands could touch my clit and pull pleasure through my body. He coached my hands on how to touch him, to have sex without its dreadful consequences. At first I felt nothing but fear for his strange curve of flesh; he seemed almost animal, his penis raw as plucked turkey neck. After he went down on me for the first time, he said he wished we would hurry up and get married so we wouldn't have to be animals. I had never had such ecstatic pleasure as his tongue licking me. My body began to cool at his words; inside my womb a core of stone hardening.

Now I lie in your arms, the morning sun blinding our just-opened eyes. You say over and over, last night, this morning, "Marry me, honey. I'll treat your heart with love and kindness. I'll be so good to you. Will you marry me?" I smile and say, "Ask me again sometime." You say, "I'll possess you in two ways only, socially and in bed. You'll go out with a wedding ring on your finger. Will you wear it reluctantly, or happily?" I smile and say, "Happily."

I don't know if you are playing with marriage the way you play with me with your cock, the dildo slid into the leather-and-elastic harness, slid into me, the arc of your hips turning inside out my ideas of sex and love. This time, after I slip on the condom, I watch your face as I stroke lubricant on the cock's head, along the shaft. I see you lick your lips and moan. Your stomach jumps. You are turned on by my finger on your cock. You say later, "If I'm going to put something this big and heavy in a woman, I'd better be able to feel it." I love the appetite in your luminous soft face, your delicate lips, the secret knowledge of your cunt folded in its golden hair just under the heavy shaft of the dildo, your clit with its tongue out waiting for my breath. You slide on your knees between my legs. You slide the heavy weight into me. I take you in one devouring moment.

Later you say, "What am I going to do? We're already acting like we're married. Don't you feel it, honey? But you haven't said 'Yes.'" You are not talking about the hard pulse of you still inside me but of something created between us where our skin meets, where the lengths of our bodies join. What am I to call this if not marriage? My ringless hand rests lightly on your back as you groan and push a little deeper into me, my cunt biting sweetly into your cock.

ENGAGEMENT RING

In your city, at a New Year's Eve party, I make my goodbyes. A young butch in a sleek black suit and black tie, smiling, courtly, takes my left hand, kisses it, says, "Always a pleasure." My left hand is bare. Tonight I don't wear the little rhinestone and aluminum engagement ring, one-size-fits-all, that you gave me on Christmas Day, hidden in the silliest romantic way in a matchbox. You said the shop it came from sold "holy things, both sacred and profane." You said, "Marry me. I'll be the husband you've always wanted." Now at the party our hostess friend, giddy with happiness, flashes an antique diamond ring, while we joke with the woman next to her about weddings, while I bless my thin, fragile circle, already crumbled in a household task. I bless again how you possess me, the absolute, dissolving gesture. Some days later you come to me with a small brown envelope and spill the contents, sparkling seeds, across my upturned palm, half-dozen brilliant rings, for any time I fancy to mark myself as yours.

Somewhere in an old tangle of jewelry is the gold circle from my first marriage. He said, "You don't really want an engagement ring, do you?" When we went to buy wedding bands, he forgot the money, so I wrote out a check. When I grew ready to leave him, he said, "My wife," his hand on my ring, stretching it until it coiled around me like rope. You say, "I'll be more of a man for you than he ever was—and more of a woman, too," and you laugh.

Husband has meant: a man who marries a woman and manages her, like livestock. Now I go back before this to one who cultivates a life with a woman, who dwells freely with her. *Wife* has meant: a woman who lives within a man's life. The last time I named myself *wife*, my own name was eaten, the house was not mine. Now I go back before this and call myself: the one with whom you wish to dwell, the woman in the house, the hidden, the veiled person, turning and twisting around your rooted steadfastness. The arch over the entrance to the house will spring up from sparkling seeds. Two vines embracing, each winding its own way, to the right and to the left, spiraling not into a tangled thicket, but into a twist of leaves and flowers that will outshine emeralds, rubies, diamonds. That will someday fade and fall into a drift of crumbled humid decay.

NEW YEAR'S EVE

On the subway platform, you lean against a pillar and kiss me. We talk idly, waiting for the next train; we've already exited one that was unmovably crowded. After a drunk man behind us began to mutter and elbow, you said, "Let's get off this ride from hell," and we rushed out at Christopher Street. You say you've learned to obey your instinct for trouble, the feeling that on nights like this a fistfight could break out at any moment, and there we would be, startlingly *there*, so obvious, but obviously *what*? You in your sports jacket, white shirt, and tie; me in a silk skirt, flimsy blouse, sparkling glass jewelry at my neck and ears. In the crowded car when I put my head on your shoulder, with your arm around me, people stared at us. Curious to be so conventional in dress and to draw so much attention. Something too intimate and queer about how we do maleness and femaleness together in public. Perhaps it's easier for you to slip through if you're not with me. One glance and you're a gay man to them or a slightly ambiguous boy. But when you're with me, I see their eyes flicker: If he's gay, why is he with her? Why is she with him? If they are two women, why do they look so much like a woman and a man? What are they up to?

A crowd of young women, with one or two men, come through the turnstiles, down from the Village. They are young enough to be my children. One has a long waterfall of brown hair, and a pale face bright with red lipstick. She wears a blue pinstripe man's suit with a tie. I say to you, suddenly and meanly, "You know what makes me angry? Heterosexual women who dress up as men, playing at being butch, not knowing what it's like, unconscious." You look at the young woman, say mildly, "I'm not sure she's straight. In any case, you're for freedom of gender expression, right?" Smiling patiently at me, you lean against a steel beam, your shirt unbuttoned halfway open, your white T-shirt stretched tight over your chest. "And I don't think it's possible to cross-dress even once in this culture and not think about it. But people are uncomfortable with the bringing together of opposites. You tell me that in the old bars there were femmes who often dressed exactly like this woman, and some butches hadn't liked it either." I wince and agree that yes, I'm uncomfortable with her combination of masculinity and femininity.

I look up and see her laughing on the platform, getting away with it, playing. No one near her on the platform has raised a hand to punish her for defying *man* and *woman*. I look up and see myself fifteen years earlier, sitting in my classroom on the edge of my desk—short hair, jeans, flannel shirt, a gold hoop in each pierced ear. In the hall the other women teachers walked by in neat print dresses, in beige skirt suits. My students eyed me, a woman dressed more like a man, who therefore looked like a lesbian to them. One day when we were discussing the women's movement, a student actually risked the request: Could we talk about lesbians? But I said nothing, too scared because other women at the school, in positions more powerful than I, were being fired with this accusation. No words to tell my students about that, or the children taken away, or the threats of violence. No way to say, *Any woman who steps outside the confines of womanhood will be called a lesbian.* Some days I taught my class wearing 82nd Airborne parachute pants, a thin pink blouse, an orange ribbon threaded around my collar. One way to express the puzzle of how to be a woman who had broken out and was clothing herself as she fell into the future, pulling on pieces of maleness and femaleness as she whirled through the air. One day my department chair called me in for a conference. She had gotten complaints about how I dressed.

You tug on my hand and say, "Get ready to jump in." The train arrives with the shriek of sharpening knives. I leave behind on the platform the young woman who flaunts herself in extremes of man and woman, defiantly standing between opposites that would grind her to nothing. I take my anger and step into the car. The doors snap together, and eyes immediately follow you and me. The other passengers begin to wonder about what kind of woman, what kind of man we are. Are we getting away with some illicit pleasure, some forbidden game that they will never get to play?

LUNCH

I am sitting in on lunch at the deli where you are meeting with a new acquaintance, and I am struggling with my pronouns. She is a big woman, over six feet, with a pulled-back ponytail and a sweet face. She is a woman with a spouse of fifteen years and four children and a life that started out as male and is now being lived as female. "At least," she says, "I am more that than I am a man." The inadequacy of the words. The duality of pronouns. She is talking to me about you, a narration of a moment on the phone with you, "So I said to *him* ..."

This is not a man passing on the street who sees you as a man, arm in arm with me, a woman. This is not a lesbian who watches us dancing at a party, and sees you as either a butch lesbian or a woman trying to be a man, and me as femme or deluded. This is someone who lives in a world where gender and sex are fluid. Not an academic exercise, but what she tells the kids about who she was as their father. The shock to me of *you* sitting here as *him*, at this ordinary Formica table, though of course that is the pronoun that suits your masculine spirit, short hair, Oxford shirt, men's slacks. The word spoken about you, not in hostility or misperception, but because, for you both, that is how flexible gender is.

Meeting you for the first time over curried chicken and *masala dosa*, she is socially appropriate to refer to you as *him*. Meanwhile, you are saying that you are a woman and transgendered, that your masculinity is a range of gender expression that should be available to all women, as femininity should be to men. You insist that you are *him* and also *her*. When I enter the conversation, I call you both by your given names to be respectful. The either/or pronouns suddenly are the jaws of a steel trap snapping shut on infinities that exist where body, self, sex, gender, the world, and lunch intersect.

The fluorescent light brightens in the little deli, as if a cloud has shifted from the sun. Your words become sharper and more distinct, someone turning up the volume on a radio. I see and hear the bothness, the severalness of this moment, a chaotic heightening of sense very akin to my first look at who really lives under the rigid grid of *black* and *white*. In a long-ago meeting of first-grade parents, every person was a woman of color except me, except some of them were almost as light-skinned as me, sitting there worrying about their children like me and like the women who were darker-skinned than us. Then later, in the city, I met proper Black ladies walking home, gloved and hatted, from church. Their profiles, lips pursed, were exactly those of my aunts. And even later I learned how the laws of race and property had been laid over us, the bodies of some white men had lain on us, reproducing *white* and *black*, producing *owner* and *owned*, to divide our lives.

Over the clatter of the lunchtime rush, she says that she did "the femme thing" for a while to prove she was a woman, but now she believes in not denying her past. In the past I have denied I was a woman. The pronoun *she* was a trap set by others to catch me. I watch her talk, cheeks flushed pink, eyes gleaming silver and green. I imagine wrapping womanhood around me like a length of shimmering metallic cloth. She looks at me frequently as she talks, careful to divide her attention between you and me. How my aunts talked to me as a little girl, curly-headed and new in my mother's arms. No words from them to me without sex or gender.

Suddenly I see you and me and her on the edge of town, a place out of my view when I was growing up, like the Quarters or the Milltown, but this is another kind of gathering. It is a world of those the world casts out, calls freaks, the women-men of the sideshow at the circus, seen as tawdry, pitiful, hidden, wasted, walking their path of reeking sawdust between the tents. Except the people there have lovers, marriages, children, poor-paying jobs. They have marigolds in pots, they play the harmonica, they write books. You live there, and now I live there too, with those who know they are both *man* and *woman*, those who have transmuted one to the other, those who insist they are neither. Outside the pegged tents people stand and peer in at us, no words for us, though just by stepping over the ropes they could join us. I could cross back into that staring crowd and be without question a woman amusing herself, Sunday afternoon at the carnival. But I would rather stay here and talk to you in this in-between place, sitting with a friend, our food spread out, savory, spicy, on the table before us.

PAINT

At the store with a giant blue can on the roof, we are buy-ing paint for the walls of our new apartment—Lemon Meringue Yellow, Faintly Pink, Navajo White, a five-gallon bucket of Semigloss White, with two gallons of Tile Red for the bedroom floor. We pay with my credit card, close to max-ing my limit, but no other choice. You've got no checking ac-count or credit from years of no money and not one piece of picture ID. The application forms have no place for you who will never fit into the either/or box of male/female. You say how much easier it is to have my car and wonder how many trips by city bus this paint would have taken. We are both relieved to be moving. Me away from my big house where there's room but always my roommate, no privacy. We whis-per our lovemaking. And you away from the chaos of a single room piled with papers and books. You're always lifting and sifting stacks, looking for something misplaced, your watch, a xeroxed article, the lubricant. You say, "Soon we'll have a home together. But someone like me—I'm never going to have much money."

In my kitchen, during our first meal together, you told me about leaving home at fifteen or sixteen, as soon as you could get a job—the apartment with no electricity, cooking your hotdog over a candle, a kid's attempt at housekeeping. Now you're sick of moving, some years as many as a dozen times for different reasons. You lose your job and apartment when technology makes you obsolete, as the computer re-

103

places the typesetter. Or people in the building look at you and say, "There's something funny about him. Her." And the harassment starts.

The wrinkled white salesman at the paint store is smiling a question to me about you. He falters and swallows his pronouns. "And your, uh, uh, uh—" I glance at you and say, "My honey?" "Yes! Your honey got the nylon brushes?" Later you say, "Maybe he thought I was your husband or your son. But maybe he read me as woman." You explain to me that you're more careful the closer you are to where you live—no *Mr.* or *Ms.* on your mailbox. You need home to be a refuge from threat on the street, not a trap where violence waits. Today you say you've always started life in a new apartment with a fresh coat of paint. I don't ask you if you've ever had to live on the street.

On the Metro bus one morning, the man smells so bad no one will sit near him. People get on, pay their fares, walk grimacing past him, flapping hands in front of faces. He had swept onto the bus without paying a fare; the driver didn't say a word. A skinny little white man, he has the imperial manner of a drag queen. He has sandals on his bony feet with leather thongs wrapped around his hairy ankles. The rest of him is wrapped in plastic cleaning bags and newspapers. He is held together with string and rubber bands. Protected from the staring world, he stinks, and we stay away from him. He mutters to himself, mad royalty in exile, and struggles with the knotted strings around his knees. Suddenly he gathers himself and his paper bags, orders, "Here!" to the driver, who stops abruptly, no bus sign in sight. He exits in his own grand, arbitrary way. I am left behind on the tilting bus to imagine the deaths'-head violence that has so pursued him that he winds himself in burial rags and wanders like a creature in search of a grave to hide in, wanders in the land between man and woman, no place to safely lay his head.

The roar of the New Jersey Turnpike arches high over us as you and I load the paint cans in the car and drive toward our new home. For months I've been driving from my city to you on that road. Some nights, late, it would blur in darkness and tears; it became a highway I traveled years before. Driving to see my children, I made fourteen-hour trips over mountains in smoky night fog, in the whiteout of a snowstorm, in the gloss of summer sun. Some trips I would sleep in a motel parking lot for a few hours to save money and time, to get to my children. They were forbidden to be in my home because I was what a woman shouldn't be. I was too much woman, I was not woman enough. I was too interested in women, in sex, in my own sex. No home for me, though my job paid the rent. No home except loneliness, living in the in-between places.

Now you say you will hold me every morning and every night in our home. We pant up the stairs, hauling the paint cans hand over hand, into the bedroom wide with sunlight, with windows full of the opulent city and the toiling river. You say that every night you will roll over and hold me, whisper in my sleeping ear that you love me, while urban lights stream like a galaxy of stars seen from a dark backyard. Every morning I will turn to you in the gray first light, and you will say, "Good morning, angel," while city skyscrapers loom like a distant mountain range in the smog. We will wake in the light of a new creation, as if we have walked back into the garden, to have a room shadowed with trees of hibiscus and palm, a bed where we can briefly lie, side by side, with only the sunlight to clothe us.

COOKPOT

We're sitting in a landscape of muted blues, pinks, yellows, squares and diamonds in mottled patterns, my grandmother's quilt spread out on our bed. You've come home with a present for me. You say, "Close your eyes," and then you begin to read: "Once there was a little girl named Daisy ..." You've found my favorite book from when I was little. The girl is given a steamroller that she drives around her town and flattens into shadows a pig that won't move, a policeman, her teacher, chickens, anything in her way. She leaves the fields quilted with sprawling fences. Back in the house with her mother and father, she enumerates everything and every person she has leveled. Then they give her a giant steam shovel. She scoops up all the shadows and makes them live again.

I snuggle in your arms and say this is the best part of the book. Not that wrong is made right, but that the girl is given unquestioned power to destroy and to create. You tease my feet with yours and say, "These feet want to be working the control pedals." I tell you maybe my spinster aunt gave me that book, the first book I read where a girl *did* something. Except, I tell you, there was another story written by the same woman, about an old woman with a magic porridge pot that cooked at her command. You say, "I read that story too!"

One day a little girl, who had been secretly listening, got hold of the pot and spoke the incantation she'd heard the old woman give. Porridge began to bubble and ooze through the village. But the girl didn't have the word for *stop*. The pictures in my book showed the tiny village engulfed by glop. The town was saved only because the old woman returned from her errands with the esoteric, definitive word. I say, "Those were my favorite stories because the women say 'Stop,' or 'Cook, pot,' and then whatever they say happens." I wiggle in your arms, slide my hands onto your naked back, and gyrate my hips slowly, pushing my thighs and cunt against your thighs, heating up. "Just like now," I murmur to you, "When I say, *'Cook, pot,'* and it begins to happen."

HUSBAND

The man sitting next to me on the grass at the March on Washington asks, "Is he your husband?" as I return from kissing you, as you step down from the microphone. Onstage, a drag queen in beaded white chiffon is ferociously lip-synching and tail-switching an answer to the introduction you have given her, praise from a drag king resplendent in your black-on-black suit. In the audience, I hesitate over my answer. Do I change the pronoun *and* the designation of *husband*? Finally I reply, "Yes, she is." He hesitates in his turn: "He hasn't gone through the operation?" The complexity of your history crowds around me as I mentally juggle your female birth sex, male gender expression. I say, "She's transgendered, not transsexual." Up on stage Miss Liberty is reading with sexy histrionics and flourishes of her enormous torch, a proclamation from a woman who is a U.S. senator, a speech that trumpets and drums with the cadences of civil rights. The man blinks his eyelashes flirtatiously, leans toward me, whiskey on his breath, waves his hand at his companions, "We're up from North Carolina." Then, femme to femme, he begins to talk of your beauty: "He is perfect. If I ever wanted a woman it would be someone just like her." With innuendo and arch look he gives truthful ambiguity to what he sees in me, in you, something not simply about "gay rights." The queen whispers in my ear with his sharp, steaming breath, "Don't let her get away. Hang *on* to him."

IV.

"STANDING AT THE EDGE OF THE DARK FIELD, MY OWN BODY STRETCHED WIDE ...."

LIPSTICK

I break an egg into the metal bowl and throw the broken brown halves in the trash. My new femme friend sits in the kitchen and keeps me company. I ask, "Do you and your lover play at sex?" I'd been telling her about phone sex with you. I'd asked what you wanted me to do when I had you in my hands, and you had said shyly, almost unintelligibly, "Make me your butch." Rocking back and forth in her chair, my friend says, "Tie her ankles and hands with ribbons, then tease. They have to maintain so much control. They want to give it up, but they don't know how." The way you brave every day, charming and implacable by turns, the blows you will tell an audience about as a political lesson, but the exact wounds hidden even as you lie in my arms. There is almost nowhere for you to be and not be watching, except in my arms. She says, "Lipstick, dark, and make her count every place you kiss. And that black silk kimono—you can use the belt. Put your hair up like a woman, stop in the middle of making love, and ask her to do something for you." I say, "This looks like power and domination from the outside, but that's not what it is from the inside." She says, "No, everything looks different from the inside."

Later, in my bed, I hold your hands over your head. The muscles in your forearms are taut as I hold against your strength, as we both struggle briefly with a woman forced to submit. Desire is a tangled knot, the past pulled and strained in us by touch. I ask you what you want, what net of desire can hold you. I slide my hands down your arms and say, "Turn over." I run my fingers across your back, the cool textures of your skin. In my hands you are rare as a mother-of-pearl shell brought up whole and closed from the river. Through its brown bark skin, iridescence shines. Its layered curves are whorled and nubbed by storms and currents, each fragile layer some protection from the waves, the buffeting years. I trace the curves of your back as you sigh with pleasure. I lie down with you, jubilant, content, as if, at a sandy verge, on the water's edge, the one wish of my life had been cast up at my feet by the waves.

RIVERBEND

You whisper in my ear, disembodied voice in the phone, calling from your house three states away: "You'll be shy when I see you." I say, "I'll always be shy, a little, at the beginning." You say, "I'll have to take you down to the river bend and ask you for a kiss." I've told you about the river, the wildness flowing right through my town, the dirt pull-offs where a boy might park the car after he's taken a girl to the movies. But when you ask, I say I didn't date much then, a careful teenager taught to distrust boys instead of to know what I wanted. Instead of how to ask and get, or refuse and use my voice and feet to fight, I was taught to keep my blouse buttoned up and my feet together. I never dreamed my fingertips like silk on another's skin, or the thrill of her hand sliding over my ass.

If I went back with you now, where would I take you? Where would we go to be alone? The sandy island at River Bend, down by where the ferry crossed a hundred years ago. But there'd be too many mosquitoes. You laugh, "We'll bring lots of bug spray." I say, "You'll put your hands on my waist, then slide them down lightly to my hips." You begin to pant, wanting me: "I won't touch you anywhere. You haven't told me I can." I say, "You can see my breasts through thin gauzy fabric. You can put your hand under." I cry out at your touch. The sand shifts under my feet. There are bits of mussel shells scattered around where raccoons come at night to hunt. The river rushes at its shoals, the mosquitoes whine, the sand is damp between my toes. It is eternally dark on the island except once in a while when a car rumbles on the bridge over us. Light beams twist into the jagged sycamore leaves. I kiss you and let my mouth stay on yours, tasting you. I hear you murmur. I tell you that your hands slide between my thighs, back over my ass. I say, "Please take me." You say, "So hot, good inside you." I say, "Please come inside me, baby, please." And you do, softly pleading my name.

You mutter, "So tired, so tired." You're exhausted from hours on the computer with no break, earning your rent, utilities, phone bill money. I say, "Now we lie down on a quilt on the sand, and pull another over us. We'll listen to the whip-poorwills and to the river rush by, and we'll sleep." I don't remind you about the mosquitoes. I don't say I hope the river lilies are blooming. Quickly, we say goodnight and I put the phone down. I fall asleep with you on the island and dream that I wake you at dawn by the rapid water. There is sand in our mouths and hair; our hands are gritty with sand. We kneel and wash our hands in the green river that surrounds us. I ask, "Let me touch you everywhere."

CAFÉ PARADISO

At the Café Paradiso, I am dining with a friend under a frieze of apples, pomegranates, eggplant, tomatoes, the bas-relief of an urban paradise, hot and loud. I am flushed as I talk of you. My words clatter like pottery slung down on the table. I tell my woman friend that you are enchanted with me in a way I don't understand, that you say over and over, "You know just how to touch me." I wish I could believe I am the most fabulous lover of women ever, but it seems unlikely. There have been the doubtful lovers who didn't want my touch after a while, and the enchanted lovers who came to me only after deprivation. What am I to make of all this praise?

I sit there with the memory of my hands as they glide over your back, light as a bird wing, quick as swallows over the nightfall surface of a pond. Holding your chin with thumb and forefinger, I run my other hand over your shoulders and chest, my fingers over your lips. My hands on you strike a spark from you, flint, hot and hotter, a fire by the water. I tell my friend none of these particulars, just how I love the maleness in your femaleness, how you are poised where the oppositions meet. You in a T-shirt and jeans, and underneath, your muscled thighs and the vee of promise folded in your pubic hair.

She, who has told me her own stories as the lover of women and of men, though not both in one, understands ambiguity.

She is exasperated that I miss the obvious: "You are not only a lesbian, but very, very queer. You love a woman who is manly, and yet do not want her to be completely man. In fact, you desire her because she is both. And how often has she found someone who really wants to touch, hold, lie down with both at once?"

As you take off your men's clothes, I do not secretly want you to be a man so I can be saved from my desire for another woman. And when I unknot your tie and unbutton your shirt, as we lie down together naked, I say with a fearless caress that I love the man I am undressing, and I also know that a woman lies beside me, not a mirror to reflect me. When we reveal ourselves in nakedness, how often you have been denied for your physical self, how often I have been despised for my sexual self. You not looking like a proper woman, me not acting like a proper woman, we have wanted the body that is *and*, that is *both*.

My friend's words to me are like light that skims across the surface of water, like a skipped rock that touches once, twice, again. Memories circle out, back, to the earliest time. My first girlfriend when I was five and she was five, me sliding down the grassy slope with her, the girl-boy I loved then. My first boyfriend when I was thirteen, as we sat on his shaded porch, his sidelong glance at me, complicit as another girl's. I've loved these contradictions for as long as I can remember, my desire that has heated up slowly over the years.

In one continuous motion, my idea of myself and who I am turns inside out, like a pond that flips upside down in the spring, when the cold winter water slides under, and the earth-warmed bottom water rises. The underlife comes to the surface. All those years I was no obedient asexual girl, but a restless lover searching for the lost garden, that place of male woman and female man. The mythic place before the Fall, before Adam was shaped from clay by Lilith, and Lilith chased out and forgotten, before Eve was torn from Adam's side and forced to lie down under him. From the beginning I have wanted you. I have wanted to sit beside you on our bed, touch you, feed you the jewels of pomegranate torn from the flesh of our lives. I have wanted to walk with you in that place where we are both at once, to lie down with you under the trees that have not yet begun to flame with the dividing sword, by the water that shimmers with heat rising, risen to the light.

SCHOOL

Morning light hot on us through the east window. Your roommate clumps up the stairs, home from the night shift, and we are waking up. You begin to stroke my breasts, and say to me, "You can't make a sound." Actually, you order me. You say unless I am quiet you will stop and count to ten. You say I will have to hold my wanting in my body. You will not let my desire run away, not even through my throat. When I gasp a little as you touch my left nipple, you do stop. And start counting out loud: "One Mississippi, two Mississippi ..." I snort with laughter, and so do you, but you continue counting, and when a little later I groan again, you stop again, and repeat the chant. You say, "I'm teaching you to make love when people are around."

I lie in your arms and dreamily remember grammar school, learning to spell the double S's in Mississippi. Which teacher was that—Miss Poag—I'd had a crush on? You nudge me gently. "This is a way to feel the intensity of desire." After a while, when I come, panting from your touch, you say, "You weren't so good at the very end, you squeaked, but otherwise you were very good." You laugh and stroke my head. I feel absurdly happy to lie in your arms and think of nothing, nothing at all but the look on your face as you watch me, as you said, "Don't make a sound, don't move." All I can do is follow your hand to a place almost like lying naked outside in the sun.

No worry about who is watching, what they will think, what names they might call me. All that forgotten in this new lesson being learned in your bed. Later, I play at school with you. I sit low on your belly, legs astride your hips, and say, "Yes, you can have me, but only if you come first. And only when you stop laughing." Later, when you lie in my arms, your head on my breast, sunlight rests heavy across us, holding us down while we sleep.

FOLDING FAN

On tour, deep in the South, I've just read from a long story about fucking, about one of the ways you make love to me. The almost all-lesbian audience and I sweat in a bookstore temperature raised to the high nineties by a summer afternoon and erotic tension. I cool myself by unfolding my silk fan while into the silence a woman asks if anyone has walked out while I was reading "those words." I say, "Not yet." Another white woman says, "We're southern, we're too polite to leave." Flirting with my fan, I say, "Honey, are you sure that's the *only* reason you stayed?" I'm in a town where twenty years ago a dyke couldn't buy a dildo, but this hadn't kept some mighty queer fucking from going on. A butch could make a harness from old belts and a dildo from pieces of a rubber glove, and a femme could scream as loud as I do under you. Maybe women want to leave now because they think what I describe is oppression, or straight heterosexual sex, or both. Out loud I add that of course penetration gets used to terrorize women, so some of us don't want it, but every penis isn't a weapon. As for whether fucking makes a woman straight, I say that when two women do it, the act *can* get considerably bent.

After the question-and-answer, I go out to eat with a crowd of femmes, to someone's home where every door is a different color and the roses on the wallpaper keep growing across

the tablecloth, where the kitchen table is loaded with canta-
loupe, blueberries, honeydew melon. One woman says that
getting others even to see her as sexual is difficult because of
the wheelchair; she remembers how scared she was the first
time she wore a red dress and waited to wheel into the dance
to be a whirling flame. Another woman says the rape took
her dearest plan sure away. Now she longs for her butch lover
to lie heavy on her, grind in her, mortar and pestle, crushing
the sweet spices slowly. She longs, but her vagina cringes, remembers violence, closes against intrusion. Another femme,
married to a man, in love with her first woman, murmurs that
everything is always better with a woman, so close, so alike,
so sweet, honey running together. I say: "Not always." I say:
"Gall, bile, the pinched fearful kisses of some women lovers."
The taste of bitterness, the honey smell of drugs, the mouth
gaping in rage.

And me afraid to walk out, not able to see why I stayed.
My skin sour with the smell of fermented apples, my alco-
holic sweat. Years until I emerged from that haze, like a heat
mirage shimmering up from highway asphalt, as if I stood in
the middle of a road, waiting for something to hit me. Years,
and then I came to lie down with you, familiar as home. Our
skin smelled clean as bleached washed clothes, dried outside
in the wind. You were familiar but strange, like my summer
backyard at night when shadows cooled the scorched ground,
and a slight dew on the grass brought back spring. You lay
between my legs and reached up to touch my breasts for the
first time. My nipples unfolded, erect, and you closed your
eyes to recite, "I touched her sleeping breasts and they awoke
like spikes of hyacinth in my hand."

PENIS

The lead Times science story is about reattaching a severed penis. A man had raped his wife repeatedly until, when he finally slept, she castrated him with a kitchen knife and threw his penis into a field. After he fled to the emergency room, she called the police to tell them what she had done, where she had thrown it. They recovered the limp phallus, and doctors reattached it to his stump, declaring the operation a success because he would get its "use" back.

I tell you that when I read this story, this is what I see: *It is night, and police and state troopers, all men in full uniformed regalia, walk in pitch blackness up and down between loud rustling rows of corn. Each one is stalking down a narrow aisle where the dirt gives under his feet. They can't tell where any other man is, and so they are alone and surrounded. They have huge heavy flashlights that shine like spotlights on the muddy earth before them. They advance with drawn guns, and with a terrible fear that they will step on their own flesh, a fear that they will find something and that they will not, that they will have to hold the bloody thing in their hands.*

When I tell you this phantasm, I declare that the policemen's search for the missing penis must have been their ultimate sex-and-gender anxiety. You laugh and say, "Not for me, even when I misplace it. Fortunately, I can take mine on and off any time." Then you launch into an account of your conversation that day with a woman friend, an old political ally who knew you to be a woman; you had talked about this very incident. The two of you had laughed that the perpetrator of such violence was finally served in kind. A male friend of yours was in the room; you both reassured him that your comments weren't directed at him. He murmured, "Of course I understand. You are talking about a violent man." But he got smaller and smaller; he shrank back against the door. With a shake of your head, you say to me, "Poor guy. *He's* on *our* side. We were so angry about rape that we were joking in shorthand for a moment, as if cutting off penises would end the abuse." I realize, with a shock of recognition, how completely you feel the violence of rape as a woman. I, even I, who have touched the tender secrets of your body, sometimes see only part of you. I read the masculinity of your gestures as shorthand for *man*, and for a few seconds forget the complicated story of your woman's life.

Yet there is the night you lean back in the easy chair, legs stretched out hard and muscular, and to my lascivious glance, you reply by stroking your hand from chest down to crotch, cupping yourself a little there, the gesture of *I can fuck you.* You are beautiful to me in your smiling cocksureness. You reach your other hand out to me, as I confide mine to your grasp pulling me close. In my ear you whisper, "When will you ask me for it?" First a question no one else has ever asked me, then nothing else, only kisses. In me the old echo of another voice reverberates, "You asked for it." But now I am standing before you who will never force desire on me and never despise me for wanting it. Finally I stand at the edge of the dark field of my own body stretched wide, wondering how to traverse its muddy dangers and humid pleasures to reach you.

FUCK

I told her about my classroom discussion of the word cunt, how I speak of the goddess Cunti, the source of law and life, order and death, creatrix of the world. The one whose name is origin of *country, kin* and *kind*, of *cunning, ken*, and *cunnilingus*. How her powers and ours were divided and defamed. The power of the universe reduced to one part of woman's body, cursed on the street and at home as *cunt*. For thousands of years, the word caught and caged like our beautiful, furry, bony part. But if we don't use this elegant word, what are we to use? Do we go on saying *down there*, as if our bodies hold hell, the underworld, a place forbidden to venture? She listened, she agreed, she began to talk about *fuck*.

Which comes, she said, from a root that means to grind, to strike a blow, to hit, an inherently violent word, irreclaimable. Someone is hitting, and on someone that blow falls. She declared that, unlike *cunt, fuck* is a word that cannot be gone back to. Another word was necessary to describe what had happened when she put her thumb in my asshole, her fingers inside my cunt, as she placed her full weight on me, and pushed into me, obliterating me with her hand. (This is my narration, not hers, my description of myself.) She said that she would not call what she did with her fingers *fucking*. I admired her hand, I agreed with the remarkable effect. But what do I call that harsh and tender annihilation—*making love?*

In a radio studio, you are reading into a microphone from a story that you've written. I sit a few feet from you, and we look at each other for half an hour while your voice travels through years of beatings, police raids on gay bars, blood on your shirt, my hands on your face. Through torture for you and humiliation for me, through losing each other when the economy crashed, when political movements swept through our lives. In the story the speaker is not exactly you, the lover is not me, but as you read we live in those years with each other. When you say, "There is a pink glow of light on the horizon outside my window. I am remembering the nights I fucked you deep and slow until the sky was just this color," then it is me you are holding so tenderly. We rise at dawn from our bed whole again, or almost whole, the scars healed over from angry red to a delicate pink that we can touch.

When you finish, the radio engineer, a friendly dyke, says off-handedly, "Well, you can't use the word *fuck* on the air. Read that line again and omit it. Just pause so people will know something is left out." The government agency in charge of national communication has demanded silence: Don't talk of what power comes over, under, between people during sex, or what that has to do with the law of the land, or with the bodies of this country's people. As you begin to comply, I sit amazed in my anger at the censorship of this word. This ugly word, an obscenity that to me has meant alienated sex at best, and at worst, assault, rape, violence.

But now this word is *my* word. I whisper, "You don't have to agree. You can make *them* do the leaving out." Instantly you understand. You interrupt the engineer. You tell her if the station needs to censor, the station will have to blank the word out. Then people will know that you are not the one who fears the power of this word between us.

You are not the one who stands over me, ready to strike a blow. You say to me, "What do you want, baby? I'll do anything." I am not a stone passive in your hand, waiting for your flint. I say to you, "Fuck me now." I move against you inside the word, as you pull the cock in place over your cunt, and begin a sweet, steady churning inside me. Slowly we make something out of old pain, rocking me, rocking me, that I come all cream and butter as I move freely between your hands, fucking.

Later you talk to me about the evening we met, when you read from that same story. You knew long before you got to the line, "The nights I fucked you deep and slow … ," that you would look up at me, sitting distant in the back row. I glanced away at the word. I shrank from the rawness of your need. Was I shrinking from your need or my own?

My need, my need. To have you lie on me. To have you, absolutely attentive, whisper that you will slip your hand between my legs, part the lips of my cunt, slide your fingers up and down on my clit until my desire becomes unbearable, then part me wide with your hand and slide your cock into me. Fill me, hold me, take me, fuck me, fuck me. Your voice murmurs as you enter me, "I love you. I love you so much." You say my name as I begin to flow through the world, wide and wider. You say, "I love to fuck you. I love when you give way to your own desire." You follow me to the edge of creation, as if through a milky way of stars, an infinity of stars like clabbered cream. You follow me down the timeless pathways, where you can go only through me, where I can go only through you.

COCK

At a lesbian conference, she and I had walked past the sex toys display, not quite browsing, but looking, at black leather harnesses as slinky as snakes, at vibrators the size of pea pods and ones shaped like beavers, at purple dildo dolphins, at tan cocks with swollen heads and balls, at the pile of pseudo-penises lying detached from any body, innocent and unused. When I asked, flirtatiously, "What about a dildo and harness?" she said, "No," abruptly, and I remembered that she had once fantasized about fucking me this way and I'd said, "No," that I'd had too much penis in my life, all those married years. The truth was, I didn't trust her with a penis on; I didn't trust her not to use it to ram all her anger at me, into me. And she had never talked to me about how good she could make me feel with fucking. I had no way of being a woman who could take her cock into me without fearing she would take and give what I didn't want. Who would I be then, lying under her? Subdued, I walked on, past the little garden of sex, where every toy had a meaning if I reached out to touch.

In a night of summer heat, I stretched sweating in bed with a woman I barely knew. She and I sucked each other's fingers, delicious as melting popsicles of strawberry, mango, peach. I tongued her fingertips, delicate as licking her clit. Suddenly she slid all her fingers into my mouth, in and out, fucking my mouth, hard and harder. I took her whole hand. "As if," I thought, "it were a cock." But I'd never wanted a penis in my mouth. I gave the one cock I'd known intimately, attached to my husband, no more than a few desultory tastes with my tongue in ten married years. Now her fingers were her clit *and* her cock in my mouth. The next day, panting on the back porch as the garden parched brown in the sun, I said, "Was that the difference between lesbian sex and queer sex? Your hand fucked my mouth, but in queer sex my mouth would have held the head of your cock, biting gently as my hands slid along the shaft." She didn't answer. She laughed uncomfortably.

You kneel beside me on the bed, your cock nodding between your thighs. I tremble from hours of your fingers and tongue on my nipples. You say, very low, "This is for you, or not at all." I stroke the shaft with my fingers and palm while you shiver. I take the head in my teeth, and you bend toward me, swaying, pushing into my mouth, filling me slowly. My mouth becomes something other than the mouthpiece for my brain. My mouth ceases to think and fills with sensation, saliva. My jaw loosens. I taste the faint synthetic sheen of the dildo. I taste how you want me by your rhythm against the back of my throat.

Then I pull back and stroke your cock as you groan and tell me you will come into my cunt like you came into my mouth. I slide my fingers around the head of the cock and squeeze. Just at that moment I remember how I did this mechanically with my husband to encourage him to harden because I thought that was what he wanted, what was necessary. I see my hand then, as if detached from my arm, going through the motion, a wind-up doll's gesture. Was he groaning? I can't remember that, or any sensation at all. I was doing it for him, no need to feel.

Now I feel tenderly toward this wobbly extension of you, held tenuously in place by an elastic harness that we've already used so much it's begun to stretch and ravel. I stroke your cock as if I'm running my hands along every inch of your skin, your sensitive back and your wide shoulders, your thick calves with soft fur. I touch you, I tell you that you are the one I want to take me, penetrate me, consume me. You are the one I want to come inside me so I can open around you, so you can ride me when I spread my wings.

You watch me as you thrust, slow, careful that I am going where I want to with you. You bend between my legs, your face almost stern in concentration. You listen to the tip of your cock inside me, to the sounds deep inside me, like the song within an embryonic bird—no, more than a viscous yolk in a brown-speckled shell, not yet broken open. Listening for the song buried deep inside me, the high-pitched singing of the heated earth, like a twist of magma pushing between the granite foundations of the world. Your cock opens into that place, the underworld. Your listening face waits for the earth to heave up under you and almost throw you off.

Under you, I watch your eyes, all I have to cling to, that hold me steady as my body becomes molten, all words melted down into sensation. I become nowhere and everything as you tell me over and over that you love me. Thought dissolves, thought turns to feathers of ash rising from a fire. I am nothing and everywhere as I carry us into the depths of my body.

MIMOSA

I can see a smear of rose dawn through the tent window when you kneel between my legs. I guide your cock inside me with my hands. For a second I feel cool inside and out, cool breeze on my arms, cool silicone dildo sliding over labia, vulva, vaginal muscles, and skin. You press deep, resting your full length on mine, surrounding and penetrating me with love. I begin to cry, to be so filled by you, without the cringing and fear that once rode inside me at this moment. You have come inside me because I have asked you to. You begin rocking inside me.

The birds are chattering. A mockingbird is floating the doublets and triplets of song over us. The sun begins to heat the air of our domed tent. Sweat slides from your chest over my breasts. You heighten my desire with your stroking, stroking, and after a long ecstatic journey, after what you later tell me is perhaps an hour, I come to orgasm from your fullness, from your glancing against my clit. Again I begin to cry, wrenchingly, as you rest on me.

In ten years of marriage to a man, I never came to this, from the pleasure of him inside me. There was always elaborate manipulation of me by him, contortions of fingers, penis, always the fear of possible pregnancy, always his fear of me. But you are excited by my desire, close to orgasm yourself. The birds have subsided into whispers. A sudden rain shower rocks the tent in the sun, and I lie safe in your arms.

You are a woman who has been accused of betraying womanhood. In my groans of pleasure from your cock, perhaps some would say I have betrayed womanhood with you, that we are traitors to our sex. You refusing to allow the gestures of what is called masculinity to be preempted by men. Me refusing to relinquish the ecstasies of surrender to women who can only call it subservience. Traitors to our sex, or spies and explores across the boundaries of what is man, what is woman? My body yawns open greedily for what you are not afraid to give me.

We dress and unzip ourselves from the tent. Walking down the red dirt road muddy from rain, in the sharp morning light, we pause to caress the mimosas of the sensitive plant, to draw our fingers along the tiny ferny leaves, to see them fold up instantly, a spasm of motion at our touch.

V.

"TO BE A GIRL WHO HAD YOU FOR HER FIRST KISS, HER FIRST EVERYTHING …."

PERFUME

House party, lesbian porn videos in the basement, and the butch I stood next to, watching, said, "Why does *every* woman in these videos have long fingernails?" All the women fucking femme to femme on the TV video were white, but the party was thoroughly mixed, the dance floor rocking with the sway of African-American, Latina, and white girl hips. Upstairs there was a birthday cake with purple sugar roses and a game being played. A cluster of femmes rated candidates one to ten on a butch scale. One butch who professed ignorance about "roles" was pulled protesting into our circle in her tight white undershirt and jeans, the keys at her belt jangling. She was awarded a ten and wandered away, bemused. A femme explained to me pedicures, stretching out her polished nails, hand and foot, like a luxurious cat. She and I looked down and noted that all the femmes had shed our shoes and were walking around barefoot, while the butches were still neatly shod in loafers, boots, or sneakers. My date got a lower rating than she thought she deserved and demanded to be upgraded; she was granted a ten for butch arrogance. One woman threw her shoulders back, swaggered her breasts, and proclaimed that she was a femme "with butch attitude."

Downstairs, to "Real Love," I danced with a friend in a see-through slinky blouse that showed off her breasts. We moved loosely, eyes accepting eyes, not looking to the side or down, but knowing who we danced with. She showed me how to work my skirts, stirring heat up around us. She told me she had a new perfume, spicy lemon: "So that when I sweat, I'll smell irresistible as fresh-baked poundcake." She urged me to buy the gardenia oil I'd been considering. Our dates were sitting this one out, two square-shouldered women in slacks and loafers side by side on the frumpy plaid sofa. I began to flirt with my friend, wordlessly, letting my eyes linger on her silk-stocking ankles, on her powerful hips clearing a space around us, on the profusion of her coiled dreadlocks and pendant earrings. I glanced at some bit of her womanliness, then at her eyes, a visual kiss of appreciation. Soon we began to laugh so hard that I said, "They are going to come over in a minute to see what we're up to." And at that moment our dates squeezed through the crowd toward us, slightly anxious looks on their faces, as we danced call-and-response with each other, just beyond the reach of their hands.

HANDCUFFS

In spring night air she and I lay in bed, overnight in a strange city, a strange room, with a red woman power poster fisting on the wall. We kissed, we wrestled. I tested my strength against my first woman lover. Her vaporous dyed-blonde hair blew in my face. I grasped her soft white forearms, her muscled soft upper arms. Her neck ridged with muscles, metal bands, as she held me down. She was stronger than me; I hadn't known that. Not a word from her, not a word from me. We tumbled over and over, my legs as strong as hers, but I couldn't get my upper body free. I couldn't get my wrists out of her hands. While I lay flat on my back, her hands pushed my hands into my breasts. She grinned silently. She didn't want to ask; she wanted to win. I turned my face and bit her hard on one wrist. She cursed and released me. My teeth left a white semicircle on her tan arm, quickly fading scars. Not a word from me, not a word from her, as we got out of bed.

In the summer, I stumbled and fell to the floor as my husband threw me out of our house. I put my hands up over my face as he shoved me into a corner. In the summer, in karate class, the instructor blindfolded me: a street-fighting exercise, strike out as soon as touched in a dark alley. Seconds passed until his arms hugged me like an iron hoop. Then my right foot kicked back quick into his right knee. I stood for five minutes in the dark. I waited for another attack, not knowing he was bent over, gasping, in the corner of the dojo.

Another lover asked what I liked in bed, and I said, "Rough sex—what some lesbians would call rough—fingers up inside me when I'm excited. I don't think I'm ready to get tied up *yet.*" At a women's festival, she'd wandered past a tent with sex paraphernalia. A pair of handcuffs glinted in the sun. She told me later she realized with surprise that she would do anything to give me pleasure, though she didn't know what that might mean. She covered me with her weight as I lay face down on the bed, my hands up by my head. She didn't hold my hands down. I wanted her to, but I didn't ask. My sudden heat as she lifted herself away from me, against the chilly autumn air, and from not knowing what would happen next. In San Francisco, I found a present for her, a red silk box with two steel balls inside, enameled over with dragons. The proprietress rolled one chiming in her palm, the sound inside a dragon egg. She said, "This is for strengthening the hands." But I did not send the present.

You are washing my car in the backyard in bright spring sunshine. You spray me with a cold thrill from the hose and I wrestle you for it, slip out of your muscled soapy grasp, out from between your upper arms hard as the weights you shift and lift at the gym. I slide and loop my hands around your wrists and forearms, point the gush of hose at you. Gasping, we call a truce, and you say, "You are so strong, and you *know* how to fight. I'd never be afraid for you on the streets." In the night, candlelight, you bend over me, breathing, "I want you to feel the lightest touch." Grasping my wrists, you say, "Turn over," and I do.

CAMOUFLAGE

I walk around the room, practicing how to move in one of the two skirts I own, the soft blue jersey with white suns. I haven't worn a skirt, on the streets or in the house, for almost fifteen years, since I decided to live as a lesbian. I made an exception only for formal gay and lesbian events: Once I wore my pink chiffon '40s tea gown; twice I wore my long black '30s dress. Three times in fifteen years. But I had a pact with myself: No dresses in the heterosexual world. I wanted others to see me as a dyke, a real lesbian, wearing pants to deny men access to my body, ready to run for safety if I needed. You question me: "But how can someone know, just by looking, who anyone sleeps with? Do you mean that you dressed androgynously to lessen the chance of assault? But we know that women don't cause our rape by the clothes we wear, so what was really going on with you?" You point out a photograph, me in a wool plaid jacket and camouflage pants, in animated talk with another woman at a demonstration. I was wearing the disguise in which I attempted escape from the country of cornered women. You say, "No matter what you wear, you still move like a femme."

I have the skirt on later as I stand at my kitchen stove, fixing supper. You come up behind me, run your hands down the fluid material and back over my hips. You slip your hands forward and grip my thighs, pull me back as you grind your pelvis and cunt hard into my ass, a pulse of fucking. I bend forward slightly, sink my hips into you, shove my hands for leverage against the stove's steel edge. I smile as I feel your hands discover nothing but skin underneath my skirt. You pull me down, and the white suns flare out on the blue around me.

Walking fast up Broadway in noon heat, on my way to meet you in the city, I'm enjoying the cool swish of my skirt, the small oval of shade cast by my straw hat. I've missed my body's sensuality I dared not show, afraid to be seen as too much of a woman in public. Now I've decided to dress as I please. Last night I'd wished for my hat when I was walking down a side street and a van pulled up beside me. The driver was someone who thought one glance at a skirt allowed him to own what's under it. He cruised by slowly, making kissing sounds. This happens sometimes even when I wear my wide-brimmed hat, but I hold my head up higher, and in the crown is stuck my grandmother's tortoiseshell hatpin, with its six-inch shaft. Men might look at me and the hat, but they don't usually slow down. Today, under my summer hat, I walk in the space I create around me. I move down the street inside the wind of my skirt. I pass through hundreds and hundreds of people, and then, at 34th Street, I see a young white woman standing on the corner, punked out in a steel-studded leather jacket, spreading the blades of a black lace fan. She has pulled her hair back in a French braid and threaded it, not with ribbons, but with copper wires. Blue rose tattoos run up her muscular forearms, and her stockings are roses woven into black lace. Steel-spiked bracelets are her thorns. On the crowded corner, she slowly, slowly unfolds her fan under the glaring sun.

140

THE RITZ

Just before we sleep, I stroke your back and begin a favorite fantasy, how we met each other when we were very young. Outside the Ritz movie theater, in thick summer night, I am a slightly plump teenager, self-conscious in white short-shorts and sandals, waiting with friends to see *Pillow Talk* or *Where the Boys Are*. You are a stranger, the only person no one knows. ("What am I wearing?" you say. "Blue jeans, and a white T-shirt, and sneakers." "Yes! How did you know?" "I do know you," I say. You murmur, to yourself, "Did you *really* have on short-shorts then?") You flirt with me in front of everyone. (And in the present, you begin to talk to me: "What's your name? What a *pretty* name. Will you take a walk with me?")

The other boys and girls have done nothing but tease me about my name since we all began school together when we were six. Suspicious, they watch me on the edge of something dangerous, talking to a strange boy, in the spill of light from the street lamp. Junebugs skid through the air and thud into us. Doris Day's poster face, virginal and blonde, smiles secretively at us. I watch myself looking at you, wanting what I can't even name. I ask you, "Are you really a boy?" And you say, "Yes. ... No." We pay our fifteen cents to go sit in torn vinyl seats. You want to put your arm around me, but I say, "No, everyone is watching. Around here, that's almost the same as getting married." You hold my hand instead and whisper in my ear how sweet I am. I say, "You are too nice to be a boy." Sometimes when we play at being teenagers, you coax me, "Please let me touch your breasts," and my nipples heat up and then flare out in the fear of being touched. Then I begin to cry, bitter hot tears, wanting so badly to be a girl who had you for her first kiss, her first everything.

Of course I knew the preacher's handsome son had a reputation for wildness, but then he said hello just to me with a smile at the square dance at the VFW, as the fiddle shrilled, and the grown folks, even my parents, swirled and stomped in the sawdust, in a vortex of arms, prancing legs, arched necks, gleaming eyes. He asked me out once to the Ritz. He was sixteen, so afterwards we sat in his car in my driveway and kissed. His mouth and hands began to lead me toward some new motion. He asked me out once more, to a baseball game. We didn't talk about anything until we sat outside my house again, and I put my face up for a kiss. Then he said, with cold purity, "I've decided since last time that I will only kiss the girl I plan to marry, who will only kiss me." What was I supposed to say? I walked into the house with footprints on my back and dirt in my mouth. The next I knew he was seeing another girl, who looked more like Doris Day, but he didn't marry her either.

One evening I did meet a strange boy at the Ritz, a friend's cousin visiting for the summer. Sixteen by then, I had my mother's car. I leaned over from the driver's seat and he kissed me, ran his hand down my ass, the first of that, the thrill of danger. Then after he left town, my friend, his cousin, wanted a date for the movies. At the end of the evening he took me to the runway for the town's one plane, blue lights along the edge like some sleazy bar, where he pulled at me with clumsy hands, assuming that I was in heat for any of them. He quit when I said, "No." I started carrying a nail file in my pocket the once or twice I went out with others.

In the fall the cousin came back to be my date for homecoming weekend. Prim in my Peter Pan collar and plaid skirt, I waited in the foyer as he checked himself into the Tide Motel. The woman clerk on duty assumed I was there to have sex with him, though if I'd intended that, I'd have sneaked in. She gingerly poked a pink pamphlet at me, headlined *The Scarlet Whore of Babylon*. My date laughed when I showed it to him. Who knows what he intended? I never let him do more than kiss me on the mouth. I never let him touch my breasts, which by then were cold and pure, unfeeling.

PILLOW TALK

Alone in a hotel room without you, I can't sleep and stay up too late watching an interview with Doris Day, blonde and perky as ever in a blue sweater to match her eyes, but with a collar up to her ears to hide her withered neck. Her hair is gray-blonde, pulled back with a bow; her mouth is drooping with lines. In clips from old movies, her mouth opens, sings, sobs, chatters. But I see, fascinated, what held me to her thirty years ago, that mouth melting under another's mouth, just as the small of her back yielded and melted under a wider hand.

I sat sweaty-handed in the Ritz watching every one of her movies, the most risqué allowed into my town. She dreamed innocently of having illicit sex, the career woman who could take care of herself slowly being seduced past caution. She tossed her head and got flowers from Rock Hudson, whose voice mocked and caressed her over the safe distance of the phone. When he was dying, emaciated by AIDS and concealed from the world, I dreamed his face stared at me, ravaged, the face of romance from my girlhood. I had never imagined that he could be gay, that Doris Day could be a lesbian girl, or that I might be.

Instead I sat in the darkened theater and yielded under his mouth hovering over hers, and squirmed with embarrassment at her pouts, her cute anger. I wanted to be like her, and she was stupid when she gave in to sex. She was a smart woman who would not or could not give up femininity, who wanted to be handled and caressed. I was ashamed of her.

On the TV an actor says, "She was incredible, a natural, seven or eight takes, and she had to cry seven or eight different ways, sniffling like a child, boo-hooing, wailing, and each time tears ran down her face—what talent." After I grew up, I read that her husband had beaten her, kicked her in the stomach when she was pregnant. I said to myself: *There is her weakness, like mine.* I told myself to be strong, be ready to fight back, the films were fantasy, male fantasy. But I had wanted to sit tousled in nothing but a pajama top and have your adoring hand slide underneath to touch my breasts. Now you hold me in your arms, and I weep for the girl who was so ashamed of yielding, if only for a few minutes, to another's hand. You hold me and say, "Bring me your tears."

FROSTBITE

Out the window I see snow falling slowly in fat white petals as you read from your novel to a gathering of women. There are some couples, natty in suits, slinky in dresses, twenty years younger than us, and a scattering of grey-haired butches our age. At the reception I see that you can't sell your books, talk to your fans, and autograph all at once. I whisper in your ear that I'll do the selling, gather up some dollar bills for change, and hear a butch say to you, "So—you write the books, your girlfriend sells them." No one there knows me or my writing. You say, valiantly, "Absolutely not. She has four books of her own in print." I struggle to open a plastic-wrapped stack of novels. When I hand them to you to slit with your keys, one of the butches jokes to me, "You're a femme? Where're your fingernails?" Furious, I say nothing. I don't know what to say. These comments are like ones I heard in my teens, when I was living as a young heterosexual woman, and my dates wanted to know what I could cook besides toast.

Later, as we walk toward the subway, I explain that I was glad to handle the money for you this time, in the confusion, but I don't want to again. Then I tell you about the slurs. You kiss my face all over, as the snowflakes fall like wet kisses on my hair. You say, "Tell them that's the kind of remark you expect to hear from men, not from another woman. And what kind of butch are they anyway, to put down another woman?" But we both know it isn't that simple. Drifts of meaning weigh down *masculine, feminine*. How we dig out from under is unpredictable, and so is who does the digging. On the way home my feet, in their flimsy low heels, get soaked and frozen; yours are dry in sensible men's brogans. When I peel my stockings off, I see patches of frostbite and am furious with myself. A mocking internal voice says: *What silly shoes to wear in a blizzard. Just like a woman.*

When I was dressing for the evening, I'd heard a voice echo from the day before. I'd walked into a women's bookstore, out of torrential rain, in my waterproof hiking boots, and a butch friend had teased, "What kind of shoes are those for a femme?" But you say to me, "Your femme power is not in your clothes." Now I remove the layers. I strip down to the power in the gestures of my hands, the sureness of my step, the way I turn my head and ask a question. I know that clothes only shadow me. This evening I decided to walk out with vanity in my lady shoes on the ice of the worst snowstorm in decades. This evening I wanted the power of showing my feet almost bare, my hips and breasts free under thin silk clothes. Now I sit on the bathtub edge, my feet in running water that stings and burns.

LUST

On a gray morning that threatens rain, you and I arrive late at the conference on lust. We walk into an auditorium of dykes hotly discussing butch and femme, and stand against the wall like Exhibit A. I wonder what judgments are being made of me, as lesbian, as femme, leaning at the edge of the room, at the edge of almost everybody's limits, the ones who think I need a real woman, and the ones who think I just need a real man. I know how some might read my body next to yours. To them the way we look is man/woman, domination/ submission, pleasure/torture. We are icons of pornography, narratives of inequality. I stand at the edge, terrified for a moment to be so visible. I could be stripped down to nothing in someone's eyes. I don't know if I need to be afraid in this room. I don't know how much has changed in the ten years since friends stood where I do now, and other women called them *slut, smut, woman-haters* for baring their desire. Their images were quarantined. Their words were punished.

In another city the lawmakers caught sight of my poems, some delicate, some drumbeat, some gyrating rhythms of how I held my woman lover with one hand and my children with the other. They said: *Her filthy life. Her obscene words. Get rid of her words.* I resisted in public; I raged in private to a lesbian friend as we closed ourselves behind car windows in a summer rain. I said, "We told the censoring women that this would happen, that *our* images would become illegal. The State cares nothing if men kill women for video sport. We knew we would be the ones pursued: the lesbian mother, the Black lesbian, the Native lesbian." The rain thundered on the car roof; the rain streamed down the glass walls. She said, "But the women showed us our wounds, the postures of servility, the reproduction of rape and violence that must be ended." She said, "I know what it means to be touched too much, to be a child in a house where I could not save myself from touch." I answered, "I came from a house where I was never touched. My wound is the absence of touch." As we cried our bitter tears, the windows curtained with mist. No one on the outside could see us sitting close together.

Years later, in this crowded room, I have another answer for her: *Desire is like a poem. The knife can mean death and life, but whose hand holds it? The rose can mean petals and canker in the bud, but whose hand spreads it? With each criss crossing gesture the meaning of lust will shift. If we dare claim our lives as our own, we must read all the poems we write with our bodies.*

JELLYFISH

We walk through our hotel lobby on the way to the gay dance next door, you in your black suit, me in a black lace slip under a silk skirt and bolero jacket. The lace shimmers on my breast, reveals and hides my skin, white underneath like foam under waves of midnight ocean. On the towering merry-go-round of a lobby couch, a circle of white men sit staring at us, hostile, cheated of grabbing at me like a gold ring, cheated of their ride at the amusement park by the sea. Their stares kill us with each step we take across the crowded floor. They know what they see: No real man, and no real woman, but a couple of queers. I've never gone out dressed like this, breasts swollen and restless. There is no mistaking the aggression of my breasts, their arrogant push forward, demanding attention. There is no mistaking that it is your attention I want.

On the night of my first dance, I sat on the bed, corseted into a merry widow, hooked up the back, strapless in front, garters stretched taut to stockings, all of me gathered, ready for something, someone. Before that night, when my breasts were beginning to swell, I stood on the frayed carpet of our living room. I made my first statement about womanhood. I said I didn't want my breasts, and I certainly would not wear a brassiere. I said, "I want them to go away." I didn't hate my menstrual blood. The seeping between my legs could have been soaked up in cloth, hidden, buried in sand. And the smell consoled me sometimes, like going back to the same place every month, to the same curve of beach where the salty fishy air was familiar. But I did not see how my breasts could be denied. They betrayed me. The nipples stood out under cloth, erect, inquisitive, on their own. My breasts moved under my T-shirt as I walked, so that men glanced, contemptuous, obsessed, at them gliding and floating, jiggling. The man who commanded as he strode past me on the street, "Get a bra, baby." Despising my breasts.

When you first met me, you said, "I read your love poems. You never mentioned your breasts." You touched the tip of your tongue to one nipple and said, "I'm going to kiss you lightly, lightly, until your breasts feel again." I did not know they had gone numb, armor of steel, breastplate over my heart, stomach, lungs, to save me from cutting looks, slash of touch. No feeling in them unless a lover used rough touch and teeth. Now you pull me to you as we enter the dance, walking through the cavernous hall like an old pavilion by the sea. You grip my waist between your hands and sway me back and forth, seaweed in the water. My breasts move languidly under the black lace, the net scratching lightly, catching them. I shudder with each rocking wave. I anticipate the moment when I emerge, breasts bare as moonlight on the black sea, when I rise and walk into your arms, my breasts luminous and shivering as moon jellyfish washed up on shore.

FEAR

On the exercise track at the state park, I watch you jog away from me. Across the river, the gigantic mirrors of skyscrapers reflect clouds, wisps of air. Behind us in the harbor, the Statue of Liberty rears up like some huge toy at the beach. Along the road, fiery goldenrod and pearly everlasting grasses light our way. I follow you down the asphalt path, fast-walking, sometimes doing knee-lifts or push-ups. Always my eyes flick back and forth on the traffic passing. The motorcycle that just vroomed by slows, the man looks back, I tense. Will he veer toward me, will I have time to scream for you, will I be able to run fast enough? The man looks away. I keep walking. Up ahead a blue van comes even with you, and I estimate the distance to get to you. It speeds on by.

The first night we ever went out in your city, on a street corner a block from your apartment, a carload of white men careened by, screamed at you, "Faggot!" We were holding hands, I was in a skirt that swirled, but they could see we were somehow queer. The next time we went out at night, I asked you what I should do if we were attacked. We had just emerged from underground, and the city was boiling around us. We walked fast, sideslipping through the surf of pedestrians. You said, "Just don't get in front of me." You told of a lover who stepped forward protectively as you delivered a snap kick. Both she and you ended up bloody, never clear if the basher thought you a gay man or a butch lesbian. Then you say, "Do the best you can. I'll never blame *you* for what the haters accomplish."

Last week another group of men from our neighborhood went down to the Village to have some sport with golf clubs—bludgeoned two men holding hands, ruptured a throat, fractured a skull. Now I watch as each car approaches you, passes you by, then comes toward me, coming close, closer, gone. I nod grimly to the muscled white man jogging toward me with a small barbell in each hand. I breathe, breathe, do pull-ups on the bar across one bench, and catch up with you by the balance beams that we zigzag on, forward, backward, like children on a beach boogie board skimming the watery film of sand. In the car I tell you about the motorcycle rider, how I was afraid, and you confess your panic. For a moment you lost sight of me in my pink shirt. You went out to the road, still couldn't see me, and began to run. You knew I had been dragged into the ocean of grasses. You called silently to me, "Hold on, honey, I'll be there soon." Then I popped up from a workout bench, as if from underwater, not even sputtering, and you turned back to finish the course. You weren't going to tell me. Why give me your fears about what some man could do to me as a woman? I say, "I don't think I'll come here alone. Too many cars passing, always someone watching to see if this time he can get away with it." I don't tell you how I watched every moment for your black shirt and cropped blonde hair, like I do when you are swimming alone in the ocean and I'm on the shore. I don't tell you of my fear for you.

ID

I walk with my supper guest to the subway station, underneath the night shadows of the stunted sycamores, onto a street where she and I are the only people at almost midnight. We turn left at the old county jail, empty and dark, an unused graveyard overgrown with razorwire that droops like wild grapevines. As we turn, a police car pulls up across from us. Two long siren shrieks blare. We look around; there is no one else in sight. The car drifts silently on to nowhere in particular. There is no doubt; he means the whistle for us, a cop's obscene warning, what he thinks of two women on the street at this time of night, alone, without men. After I've taken her down through the station tunnels, I start home, truly alone this time, fists clenched. If he stops me, I have brought no ID with me on this five-minute walk from our apartment. And would that stop him? And would I want him to know where I lived?

After the demonstration at the Supreme Court, the police put us women in the same prison van with the men, but at the jail they separated us, lesbian women to one cell, gay men to another. While we sang to each other, they took us out, one at a time, to be identified. In the cubicle, the white policeman smiled at me through the metal grille and asked me my name, my mother's name, my home address. As he wrote up the paperwork, he said, "But what are you doing this for, someone as nice-looking as you? Want to go out with me, after this is over?" I said, "No, thank you, officer," as he filed the charges. In the courtroom, reunited with the gay men, we pled guilty to protesting a law that had declared us ineligible, too sinful, for protection under the law. After I pulled my ID and fifty dollars from my left shoe and paid the fine, I went home. That night the TV showed me singing, defiant, with the others outside the courthouse, for all the country to look at. But I lay awake fearing only one stare, the humorless look of the policeman whose thin-lipped mouth smiled at me through the steel grille.

THAW

You speak at the university in a sterile auditorium to an academic audience, in the location and dim lighting of my usual lecture. But this time I sit in the fold-down desk just being your girlfriend. I try not to clack my silver bracelets at odd moments. I feel flushed, uncertain, like myself but like a teenager. Everyone must see how I want your sure hand on my waist, your rough, sweet voice in my ear. Tonight I am not a writer behind the lectern who uses words to reveal and hide, words falling like snow into silence, into crystal flakes that reflect a small angle of my desire. Tonight I could walk through the snow naked and warm, and everyone would follow the melted prints of my bare feet.

Later that night I sleep with you in a strange, cold room. You warm me, neck to feet, with your length. Toward morning I dream: *I am in that cold room in bed, in sheer black nightclothes, sunlight over me. You (yet this is not you) sit in the kitchen with a man and then bring him in to look at me. When he leaves, you bring in two more men to look me over, and then a fourth man comes, looks, leaves. I walk out of the bedroom, wander through the building's maze, and return. I say, "What were you doing? Those men looked at me like I was your whore." The you-who-is-not-you laughs, and I get up. I walk barefooted out of the room, out of the building, into the dirt yard. I know I am leaving you.* That is when you wake me, with your arm close around me, wanting to know, "Sweetheart, is something

156

wrong?" I tell you the dream, and you say, "That was not me." I say, "I know. It was me. I am still ashamed for anyone to see my desire."

At midnight, in the bus station, I waited for a lover. I wore jeans and a work shirt and a bright red and purple shawl around my shoulders. I was flushed from my bath and with anticipation. I had nothing in my hands, no book to read, no way to pretend I was not alone. I was the only woman there when the other person waiting, a man, walked up and leaned over me. I said, "I don't want to talk to you," several times. He persisted. I repeated. Pissed off, he snapped his fingers at me, "Tighten it up, baby, tighten it up," to show the station attendant that I was his prostitute and that I would fall into line. Then he stalked out. I was a woman marked as feminine, outside the house and alone. Even if I sat perfectly still, staring ahead, he knew my body solicited attention, set things in motion. If he saw me as a lesbian, what did that matter? He looked at me and thought he saw a smile, a wink, beckoning.

The old laws said prostitutes could not walk in public places or display themselves in windows. The old laws said any woman who worked and lived alone in lodgings could have her room raided on the suspicion she was a common prostitute. The old laws said prostitutes could be reformed; they could work for no wages in a public laundry where they'd sweat and wring and learn to be good wives. The old laws said we had to wear something to show the difference between us, the whores and the wives. Some sign in our dress—sandals or headbands one year, black triangles another—when we were in public. Otherwise, when the wife went out of the home onto the street, any movement of her body could be dangerous. She would have to answer the question: Inside, outside, what was she worth?

Now some see me as a blank passivity, like snow, a white surface waiting to be molded by your hand. Some watch to see me dirtied by your tread. Others, and even my sleeping self, have damned me as *whore*. But in the beginning, when we all held each other in common like the land, when what we kept between our thighs was as precious as the earth, *whore* was a word that sparkled like water. To call a woman by that name was to say, "Dear, precious, *cara*, caresses."

I have lived exiled in the cold land of shame. Now that you are here after so many years, you hold me in your hands. Under your fingers my skin warms out of a numbed sleep where I kept myself safe. You touch my wrist, my waist. My flesh begins to ache and I come back to myself, like the melt at spring thaw, snow heat rushing down through rivers, to whirl dynamos until the mouths of dams spit electricity. Now when we are alone, when we are where others watch, I show you with the arc of my neck, the bend of my arm, a hint of where I can take us and with what velocity.

GREED

She is the last in line as I stand with four other writers, signing books at the authors' table. Earlier, while we waited for the reading to start, she watched me as I entrusted myself to your arms, and you slow-danced me across the room. In a mauve crepe dress, in black stockings seamed up the back of my legs, unmistakably to my ass, I ground sweet sex out with you in front of everyone, shock and aftershock. She stood by a clump of women who stared as if watching a crystal vase on a ledge begin to topple—falling silent water, a wreckage of peonies in a chiming of glass. Now the young white woman patiently edges forward. She shifts her weight expertly, hip to hip, on high-heel stilts, and smooths her tight black-skirt thighs. The poet on my left leans across to ask the novelist on my right a question: "What is the number of her shade of auburn hair?" Another in this row of femmes jokes to me, "Honey, you're too dangerous in that dress. Gonna have you arrested and locked up as serious competition."

When the young woman makes it to the head of the line, I see that she is tiny, only up to my shoulder. Her mouth opens, blood-red, as she says, "I've been a feminist since I was fourteen, and a lesbian always. I hike days in the wilderness by myself, I outkick the men in karate, I outhit every woman on my softball team. But when I come to bat, my teammates start to joke, 'Just undo the top button on your blouse. That should take care of the pitcher.'" At nineteen she heard the police say she must have wanted it, walking in that skirt. She asks me, "Why do I dress like this? Is there something wrong with me?"

What shall I answer her, this woman young enough to be my daughter? That in femininity we are seen as essence of woman, passive, weak, and helpless, with sex our only skill and breeding our only use? That femininity unpossessed is property on the loose, people ready to boil up the fence, to keep us from straying like cattle? That I know her moment of rage and shame, my woman's body a pot that someone else pours their despisal into?

She hands me a card, her name encircled by pansies, violets, forget-me-nots, pensées, heartsease, remembrance. Pandora's card. The woman of thought and memory. Pandora's vase of honey. From its mouth the outpouring of pleasure, at its mouth the entrance to desire. The mouth of the singer, the mouth of the poet, the mouth of the law-giver. The way of creation, the way of order and chaos, the way of death and beauty. But another legend goes that it was a greedy man who broke the vase and spilled war, pain, sickness, and death into the world. The one who saw how he could gather more than the others, the one who chose the act of rape, the naming of paternity, the ownership of her womb.

The evening is over. The empty lobby is strewn with the events programs and with newspapers. We could pick the papers up and read the current old condemnation of women—how selfish, irresponsible, wrong, and weak-willed women, promiscuous women and unwed mothers, have let loose anarchy in the nation. But of the audience, only this woman is left, and she wants only to hear from me and the other women.

The greedy-eyed women at my side, the one in lycra pants red and smooth as lipstick, the one in black velvet and leather shiny with steel. The women who have spoken out loud in defense of our bodies and our desire. Shall we tell her that every swing of our hips in this world is defiance? And it is defiance if we declare: *I decide who I touch and who touches me, I decide who I give to, and what shall come of it.* Pandora: all-giving.

KISSES

We climb down the stairs to your gym, a basement of gun-metal gray machines lined up in rows, each array of equipment designed to augment a specific segment of the body—the deltoids, the pectorals. It looks like the inside of a factory, a body factory. You say you work out early in the morning because then you can take your time. No men waiting in line for their turn while you wrestle with yourself to sweat on the weights as long as you need to. The bulletin board has a magazine picture up, a row of women with defined and staring muscles. You point to the one who is most sculpted, whose muscles are most precise, and say she lost the bodybuilding competition because she had gone too far toward masculinity. The judges preferred more blur in a woman's body. You say you want me to come with you one day as you work out, to spot you, my hand out to break and balance a slip as you lift. I say that I'll murmur, "You can do one more, baby, one more for me," while I kiss the back of your sweaty neck. But you demur: No kissing here. It's a gay gym, but a few heterosexual couples insist they can do it anywhere they please, the man and woman who rolled writhing on the mats—while the infrequent men caught at it with each other in the bathroom are always kicked out. Though we are two women, here we'd be seen as heterosexual, and resented. No, no kissing here.

In the Tastee Diner we've had our french fries and cole-slaw and a shared chocolate milkshake. Full of comfort, I put down the tip, you go pay the check. When you come back to the red plastic booth, some old '60s song is playing. You take me in your arms and begin to dance with me in the aisle between the booths and the coat rack. At the next table two women are scandalized, their eyebrows in arches of astonishment. Later you joke that they wanted to hold you responsible, to say, "Young man, this is *not* a dance hall." But I was moving with you far beyond boyfriend and girlfriend, beyond a lingering kiss taken over lunch. I was giving myself to you in the way I have perfected over the years since the summer night I stood by another butch lover, drinking beer outside the hidden back door of a small-town gay bar. Since the moment a drunk white man staggered out past us, and began to taunt me with his invitation: "What are you doing with her? Come with me. I can give it to you." Bewildered, I turned my back on him, moved closer to her, put my hand on her bare muscled forearm. Whoever she was, I was not the woman he thought me. But in daylight, in public, in a parked car near her job, she wouldn't let me kiss her.

I have waited years for you who wants to flaunt me on her arm, my face radiant with desire, as if I'd put my face deep into a lily, heavy with pollen, and raised it to you, smeared and smelly with butter yellow, sated but not yet satisfied, our meal not yet finished as I cling to you in the aisle of the dilapidated diner.

MARTIAL ARTS

Arm in arm, after late theater and midnight supper, we are on a 3 a.m. East Village corner jammed with punk hustlers and club-goers. With you in a suit and tie, me in a gossamer dress, we stand out like we're holding up a sign that says *Support Queer Rights*. Sure enough, as we step off the curb, a man behind us yells drunkenly in my ear, "Hey, they're *lesbians!*" He wants to tell the street that he can read us, that we can't hide from him. He assumes we are hiding. You spin and begin to shout deliberate, angry obscenities, while I pull at you to get out of there. You jerk your hand away sternly, tell me, "No," as the man's apologetic friend drags him off.

Across the street, I begin to cry. Too many memories of harassment when I was afraid and didn't know what to do. I'm ashamed that I wanted to run. But I'm also still ashamed of the time I shouted instead, playing basketball with a butch lover on a Sunday morning. The white man leaned his bulk over the fence to taunt us: "Dykes. Queers. Lezzies." I yelled back: "Yeah, we are! So what? Leave us alone!" Yelling at him again as I bounced the ball twice and tried another basket. Eventually he left. I was ashamed because my lover was mad at me for getting us into trouble. She'd looked frantically for a Coke bottle to break into a weapon. Why didn't I keep quiet?

You listen and say, "You weren't the one that started the trouble, were you? And of course you mouthed off, femme tactics to make a scene out of danger, to get people's attention, to get help." I say, "But I was so angry that I turned my back on him and dared him to hit me." You jostle me a little and say we have to walk on. Women who pass us see I am crying. Their quick glances read me as a woman in trouble with a man; any minute one will intervene. You say, "It's OK to be angry or to be scared, but I never turn my back on trouble."

I tell you about my femme friend, preening languidly on the couch, who instructed me in how to handle trouble. One hand twined in her hair, extravagant nails like rubies in her jheri curls, she told me that when men bothered her on the subway she just acted crazy; they left her alone quick. You ask, "Have you ever thought that you've saved yourself, and maybe a lover, by mouthing off, being in-your-face? Most bullies are cowards who leave when they see you are ready to fight."

You say, "If someone decides they want to beat the shit out of you, that wasn't started by your pride in yourself." You tell me that when police raided the Stonewall Bar, street prostitutes and drag queens screamed and used their high heels like stiletto knives. I tell you that ten years after Stonewall I stood with a handful of others in front of a county courthouse. We were lesbians, bisexuals, gay men, and we looked like dykes and sissies. It was our first demonstration. Two men had gone to a swimming hole on the river, looking for queers to bash. They had beaten a man to death with a tree branch. Our signs had read: *We aren't going to die for you. We aren't going to hide.*

You say, "You know, I think you would like aikido. You already move in that style, a flexible power that comes from balance, motion, foot play. An opponent determined to subdue you finds that his stone can't break water, that he's chasing the wind through the trees. With the curve of a hand you can defeat your opponent as you twirl him past you like a dancer."

VI.

"S/HE WHO MUST BE WRESTLED WITH OR EMBRACED

... ."

BARE FEET

The three of us—all femmes—lean forward and into each other. Our sandaled right feet extend toward the camera's eye. Our painted toenails gleam through open toes. The woman to my left says, "I haven't worn a dress in twenty years. What do you mean, you've learned to flirt your skirts?" She is sophisticated and powerful in cream silk slacks and shirt. The woman to my right says, "Honey, *I'd* like to see you work them." She is comfortable and stylish in a blue print dress, a squished flowered blue denim hat. I've known these two women for over ten years but have no idea how each struggled through to her way of being a woman.

Maybe one was taunted as "Daddy's girl" or "Jewish princess." Maybe the other was jeered as "Sapphire," or always called out of her name into that of another dark woman. Each with her own story of the rooms she grew up in, and the women she watched cook or clean or go out the door to work every day, or the men she watched leave for work. The father or the mother or the grandmother at day's end at the kitchen table, weary, hand to head in a familiar gesture. The girl in the kitchen door, head tilted and hand raised in her own already habitual gesture. Each girl with her own thoughts as she walked to school in the dress she chose or the dress she hated, being watched or ignored through gawky adolescence by the neighbors and the people of the town. Each initiated into the mysteries of womanhood, even if she did not want to be. For each, there was the moment when we were commanded to close our eyes and walk forward.

My eyes are closed because I am crying. I am eight or twelve or sixteen, and I am crying as I always do at this point in the movie, when *Gone With the Wind* comes to my Alabama town every four years. I am crying because on the screen a slender white woman is groveling on the ground. It is night and all around her is ruin—her slave-owning life of opulence gone, her family without food, the garden trampled. She weeps and digs her hands into the dirt, which I think must be the same red clay as the dirt road that goes by my house. She holds her filthy hands up to the dawn and swears: "I'm never going to be hungry again. No, nor any of my folks. If I have to steal or kill—I'm never going to be hungry again." Music swells, gauzy curtains sweep together. The lights come on for intermission, and I don't look behind and above me to the balcony where Black folks sit if they come to the movies. The ones who have had their lives and labor stolen away, the ones who have been killed for demanding food, for rebelling. I am not thinking about them at all. I am clasping my hands around my waist, so much bigger than the corseted seventeen inches Scarlett had herself cinched into.

The movie reverses us, mirror opposites: Black woman, white girl, white girl, Black woman—"Mammy," Scarlett, Melanie, "Prissy." The movie offers me two choices: Be the white girl who suffers through sex and then dies having a baby for the husband who loves not her, but his name and his property; or be the white girl who trades sex for security, who acquires her own property, who cares for no one but herself. No one in the movie acts like the Black woman who raised me, or like my mother, a white woman who worked for her living since she was sixteen. In the glossy movie poster outside the Ritz, Clark Gable sweeps Vivien Leigh off her feet. I sit up all night reading the novel to find that moment.

Long years after the screen goes blank, I see an old newspaper photograph, taken about the time the novel was being written. I see a horror: In the dim background, on bare-branched trees, two Black men are hanging, elongated, suspended like feed sacks, or like animals butchered at fall hog-killing time. In the foreground are young white men, snickering, looking (except for their clothes) like the boys I went to high school with. They have the self-satisfied smirks of boys caught laughing at a dirty joke. In the foreground is a middle-aged man, close to my father's age in my first memories of him. The man stands and looks sternly out, but one hand, one forefinger, points back to the dead men. He is warning: *This will happen to you if you take what doesn't belong to you.*

Beside him stands a woman old enough to be his mother, a white-headed white woman old enough to be my grandmother. She does not look out at the camera or at any of the other white people or at the slaughtered men. She looks up and off into the air. She seems to pretend she sees nothing. She withdraws herself, yet she is there. A few young white women look at the camera; some are giggling. Outside the frame is a woman we can not see: A white woman, lying in the dirt of her front yard, whipped into tatters for being a slut, white trash, the skirt of her dress blowing like torn paper in the night wind. Far outside the frame is another woman: A Black woman sitting on the floor beside her overturned kitchen table, food splattered on the walls. The insides of her thighs are bloody. Her eyes are fixed on the wall. Her obsidian imagination sees, miles away, everything that will be in the photograph.

When I open my eyes, rain falls on unpaved clay roads. I am a woman watching the rain unscroll stories from when I was a girl: The Black woman who was part of my everyday. The woman who walked to work from the Quarters, two miles to our house. Her ruined shoes fell to pieces in the mud, her toes shoved through gaping holes. Every month she bought a money order, and she sealed it in an envelope. She got someone else to write down the name of her oldest daughter, living in the north end of the county, taking care of a husband in a wheelchair, gunshot in the back by a white sheriff's deputy, paralyzed.

The white girl who was part of my everyday. The girl who walked to school from Four Points by the sawmill and sat at the desk in front of me in the alphabet. Pregnant, she walked ahead of me in the procession. Black-robed, she balanced a shift of weight on new black heels. Her once-slender waist jutted grotesquely out. She walked head up, married but just barely. The night I'd driven off by the river, her boyfriend's car had been parked there. She'd raised her head briefly from the back seat. Her eyes glinted, caught in the headlights' glare. No one was supposed to see. She walked across the stage; she didn't fall. The man in charge handed her the diploma and shook her hand. No one else touched her. She walked past us all, her head up.

TATTOOS

As we push the cart toward the supermarket, the livery people just outside the automatic door hustle us for business. The only African-American woman looks at your stone butch and my denim femme, then politely asks, without missing a beat, "Ladies, do you need a ride after you finish?" When we check out, the white cashier calls you "Sir." In the shopping center shoestore, when I sit down to try on sandals, an African-American woman in the next chair nudges me, smiles, points to you, and says, "Better have her hang onto your purse while you do that. It might walk out of here."

When we return from the City at 2 a.m., in formal gown, suit-and-tie, we decide to get breakfast at the freeway diner. Our waiter is a street-worn white guy in his sixties. We praise his tattoos as he takes our order. After we finish eating, he carefully waits until the two policemen drink their coffee and leave. Then, smiling graciously, he offers, "Ladies, please come back again."

In my classroom, a *Puertorriqueña* student listens patiently as five white dykes argue about the night before, the two women they saw dancing at the bar, African-American and Latina. The one who was leading, how could she be a butch? Too fluid, too expressive. The *Puertorriqueña* finally interrupts and interprets for them: The woman was leading with exuberant Latino hip-hop, a young male style adapted into Latina butch expression. She smiles, says, "Yes, of course you saw how hotly one woman followed the other. But you just didn't know how to see the place they were dancing inside."

DRAG SHOW

I've invited a lesbian neighbor to supper, and she arrives at the door with a bouquet of tiny purple asters. She's angry about something in the local gay paper. She spreads the pages on the kitchen table to show me a cartoon with three parts: A "Black Face" of a goofy white man in a bow tie, ears sticking out, his face blacked, his teeth white in a big grin. A "Girl Face" of someone with frizzed blonde hair, pursed, rouged mouth, a Tallulah cigarette holder with a prominent Adam's apple and broad shoulders, presumably a man in woman's drag. And a "Gay Face" of two nerdy people, one in an Oscar Wilde jacket with half-shaved head and a girlish ponytail, the other in an aviator jacket and scarf sporting a flat-top Philly cut. It's impossible to tell the sex of either, though their gender styles are feminine and masculine. She can't explain what upsets her about this cartoon as she sits in my kitchen, a butch woman any school child would call mannish.

I pour couscous into a skillet of hot water and steam boils up around my face. I begin to rant about why these parodies make me so angry: That it is infuriating when white supremacists who mock, hate, and have institutional power to gravely injure African Americans are compared to gay men who cross into a despised femininity for which they are condemned and often killed. That to pretend to be "the other" in order to put forward a controlling and negative idea is not the same as to embrace "the other" as part of the self.

I tell her: "When I was a little girl, the white men in my hometown, maybe even my father, used to do black-face, a vaudeville show fundraiser for some civic organization, maybe the Kiwanis Club, or maybe for the all-white volunteer fire department that took so long to find smoke and flames when a house burned in the Quarters where the Black folks lived. Once a year, grown white men got up on stage and reversed their color. They ridiculed the people who had raised them, who worked side by side with them every day. They became the opposites they feared, but not the people who lived all around them, on the other side of the color line. They denied they had ever crossed that line. They denied the others who were their distant cousins, unknown nieces and nephews, those who were their children."

And I tell her: "Once a year, when I was a teenager, the Key Club, the high school version of a local men's group, would stage a womanless wedding for its fundraiser. Anyone in school could miss a morning of classes by paying fifty cents or a dollar to watch while half the boys on the football team, dressed in suits, escorted the other half down the aisle. The other half was costumed in their girlfriends' or their mothers' pink taffeta, blue net, white lace formal gowns and Sunday dresses. The other half simpered and flirted, minced in exaggeration, cried hysterically. The hairy chests of the bride and bridesmaids showed above the grapefruits they'd stuffed into décolleté bodices. It was always a shotgun wedding. Who would marry the woman, and be her other half, if they didn't have to? Who would be a woman and suffer the humiliation of those breasts? I shrank down in my cold metal chair while some of the boys in the auditorium shrieked and catcalled their approval of this processional segregating the sexes into weak and strong, stupid and smart. Some of the boys, the skinny effeminate boys who were in the concert band with me, who never went out for sports like I never went out for majorette, those boys shrank down quietly too. It was the mid-'60s, and we girls were not allowed to wear jeans or shorts to school. This assembly was the only day of the year, except Halloween, that a boy could wear a skirt in public. And only if he agreed to ridicule femininity, even if he dreamed secretly of taffeta."

I tell my friend: "When you live between opposites, you cannot escape the s/he who will follow you, who must either be wrestled with or embraced. And I have seen the beauty in that embrace. Fifteen years later, at my first gay drag show, in the blurred eye of one spotlight, a tall melancholy drag queen lip-synched a love song. She gleamed, copper-skinned under beaded black net. She strolled the edges of the audience. Her gloved hand stretched elegantly out to touch my hand. When she leaned forward, bittersweet gardenia scent drifted across my face, and she looked directly into my eyes. I told myself then: *If she did not have to be the man he was raised to be, I did not have to be the woman.*"

HOUSEWORK

My ninety-year-old aunt leans back in her recliner and demands with friendly curiosity, "But tell me, which one of you does the cooking?" She herself hates to cook. When she was in her own home, she preferred to mow the lawn in Bermuda shorts her husband disapproved of. Since she was widowed, she's shared a home with another aunt, her younger sister, who fixes the cornbread, field peas, squash casserole for our dinner. I have introduced you as *she*. After years of rumors, I am bringing you home, without apology. You joke that you are my dead father's every fear: a working-class Jew, a Communist, an antiracist political organizer—who is also a stone butch transgendered lesbian. You are the one he feared was taking over the world, and you've ended up married to his daughter.

But my aunt is more interested in what happens to household work when two women share it. She doesn't assume I cook and you don't, or that you can use a screwdriver and I can't. She doesn't assume there is a connection between *masculine, feminine*, and who does certain kinds of work in our home. She just asks her question. Sometimes she slips and calls you "he," just like I occasionally do. There was the time, at the beginning of our life together, when you and I debated about the laundry. I wanted you to sort by fabric and colors, and you said you couldn't, you'd tried in the past and made a big mess, and I began to get mad. You said, "I'm not a man because I have laundry dyslexia." There was the earlier time we were discussing the complex politics of genital mutilation, imperialism, and race. You said, "You are talking to me as if I don't have a clitoris."

There was the time we went to the Bureau of Motor Vehicles to get your driver's license. They demanded your birth certificate, which you couldn't show them. It said *she*, and you needed a license with *he*, a piece of plastic with the pronoun that matched your looks so a policeman on a lonely road at night would not say, "You—get out of the car." The only ID you had were bills with your name and address and, from the hospital you were born in, a frayed piece of paper with your name and the genderless inkprint of your baby feet. The BMV clerks would accept none of it. I leaned against the counter, playing your bored girlfriend, while you fought through the bureaucratic layers.

Meanwhile, the people who had stood in line behind us took their test. First, the nervous sixteen-year-old white boy who'd waited with his father; then the middle-aged white man in a suit who'd stared at us until I stared back and made him look away; then a Latino with his name sewn on his overalls; then a Latina with a baby in a stroller. Each had to convince the authorities that he or she belonged within these borders. Those with white skin had almost enough proof without a single piece of paper. For those with dark skin, often no number of documents was sufficient. I got my driver's license on my sixteenth birthday; it was so easy. The examiners saw *white* and *woman,* and I fit myself without question into one of the boxes. Either *M* or *F,* either *W* or *N.* After all, the state demanded I live in one or the other. In my billfold was the document, the piece of plastic that proved I passed the test.

Finally you were handed your test, officially stamped, by a uniformed butch woman who seemed like a dyke. With an angry "Sir," she passed you through, a man making trouble, not someone who could almost be her. No room in that line for questions about what is *man*, what is *woman*. The State has a compelling interest in matters of ownership, to know which is which, a fact that has nothing to do with how we share chores in our house. But before we sit down to dinner with her, my aunt asks again, "And who does the cooking?"

EARBOBS

We've finished midday dinner at my mother's house, me and my youngest son on holiday from college. Mama goes down the hall to her bedroom and brings back a fake leather jewelry box, which she sets on the Formica kitchen table. She's taken out the pieces she still wears; I can have anything I want of what's left. My boy and I rummage in the necklaces, pins, earrings. Here is *Mother* spelled out in fake pearls; I don't remember that she ever pinned it on. Here are the pink pearl screw-on earbobs, older than me, nubbly as nipples; she wore those with her tailored rose-pink suit. Such tiny earrings for such a big woman. Nowadays she says to me, "I wear clothes that most women wouldn't." She means her extra-large sturdy men's nightshirts, her sensible shoes.

But she always dressed me like a girl, knitted my sweaters, sewed all my clothes. My favorite dress was dark blue taffeta with a black braid. I wore it the winter I started menstruating; my skin glided under the silky taffeta. She made the blue-flowered voile with a white collar that I wore the spring I got engaged. She made my wedding dress, white velvet, and the black velvet dress suit I wore home to my bridal shower. She was mad I'd put it on before I was married; I didn't understand black was for after the ceremony. She sent clothes when I was married to my first husband, his and hers jeans jackets, but I bought the yellow polka-dot chiffon maternity dress that lasted through two pregnancies. After I left him and began living as a lesbian, her presents one holiday were a pair of white pearl earrings and a plaid flannel jacket.

When my father died, she took me to their room, to his closet, and asked if I wanted any of his clothes. She expected me to want something. I chose a white cotton dress shirt, a thin black-and-red striped tie, and his summer Panama hat. Later that year, when I did poetry readings in the South, I wore his clothes. When women asked me what the hat meant, I said it made me feel powerful. Was I cross-dressing as my father, for my mother? I thought I was becoming a lesbian.

Now she sees that I've chosen dresses again and earrings. She offers me accessories. I pick up the pink pearl earbobs, and the plastic jade clip-ons, and the jet choker with matching earrings, and the fire-opal brooch my father gave her. As I set them aside, my son begins to try on earrings. He screws on a pair of white pearl and blue stone. He gets up to tilt his head this way and that in the kitchen mirror. Dissatisfied, he takes them off, and clips on gaudy green glass and rhinestone. Mama says, "You could get one ear pierced for a gold hoop. A lot of the boys do." He says, absently, "No, everyone is wearing that now," as he hands the earrings to me, and we begin to clear the kitchen table.

BOY

On the way to the airport, my oldest son relents and says I can take his photograph in the Passenger Unloading Only zone. What develops later is us smiling, awkward, next to each other, hugging in front of two bulging duffle bags. I am surprised at how much he looks like his father—older, darker, thinner, tense. We are almost a photograph of his father and me after this son was born. I am surprised because he resembled me for years. My women friends who had never met him sometimes recoiled with shock, shaking hands with me as a man, over six feet tall with the shoulders of an athlete, but with my lean legs and thick body, my wide face and high cheekbones, his gestures mine in a mirror.

When I was a young wife, I grieved as the boy I married disappeared, the boy so afraid of growing up to be a girl that he had starved his curves into bony angles. Later my son told me, "I look around and I see how the grandfathers exist in the fathers, how the things they do get passed down until a man can be like skeleton bones that move. I don't want to be like that." Now, without warning, I see in my son's thin face that his girlhood has slipped away into his manhood and is hidden for the moment, perhaps forever. But he hoists up the two bags and walks away into another journey. His strong body sways as he wrestles with bone and flesh as he balances his fugitive selves.

BLADE

When you and I begin the drive south, it's déjà vu all over again, speeding down I-95 with a husband, like twenty years ago and more, going home for the holiday. Except then, one child was tiny in a car crib, the other a toddler strapped straining in a car seat, and now they are grown. Except then, I was not with you. The son we are headed to see is about to host his first festive dinner with the woman who is now his honey. They live in neighboring apartments in a complex of red-brick buildings, like where I lived when I was first married to his father. By my son's backsteps I almost look for remnants of the daylilies I planted to try to make a home. As soon as you and I knew we were going to be together, you told me, "Now they are my children too, and I'm going to love them just that way." Today you joke with me that I'm bringing him home a drag stepdaddy, but you mean it.

The dinner is crowded with graduate students, most in their early twenties, a young queer studies crowd. We have silly dime store games as presents for our son and daughter-outlaw, water pistols, bubble toys. In the brief space before dinner, I sit on the edge of your armchair, and then on your lap. Conversation is both crowded and quiet. It's impossible to tell what the other guests think about our presence there, living specimens of their theories, butch and femme, drag king and lesbian queen.

My son and his honey are in the kitchen. He mixes orange juice to stir into the creamed sweet potatoes. She takes a last look at the browning turkey. As I put my cornbread dressing on the table, young men and young women ceremoniously carry in their specialties: twice-baked potatoes, cranberry and walnut relish. Just as we all crowd to the table, someone brings the bulging turkey out and places it at the head of the table, in front of a vacant chair. My son stands quietly in the kitchen, avoiding that place. His honey lays the carving knife down beside the bird and goes back in the kitchen. I run upstairs to the bathroom, wondering how they will solve this problem of authority, family, who is to head the table, who is to carve, who is to sit at the side. How to negotiate the metaphors of blade, flesh, communion; mother, father, children; maleness, femaleness, domination, submission. Are my son and this woman our children? Are they the parents of the others? Am I everyone's mother? And how can I be? Me who has just been making out with you by the stairs, not pure enough for a mother, too young in my flirtatiousness, and with the wrong husband.

When I return, everyone is seated but no one is at the head of the table. You are sitting to one side, next to an empty place and plate for me. But you have the blade in your hand and are slicing huge slabs of meat onto a platter. I begin to laugh. I say, "How did you end up with that?" And you say, "Don't even ask! I've never done this before in my life." But my son says, "It took a lot of courage to grasp that knife."

PALACE

At almost sunset in the formal garden we walk on plush green grass between borders of perennials—golden everlasting, pink hollyhocks, the masks of purple-black pansies—a floral arrangement as grand as any at a lord and lady's banquet. I've been telling you a story about Radclyffe Hall, who like you led a life across and between, sex and gender. But unlike you, she was a wealthy woman when she dressed in men's clothes and was called John by those who loved her most. When she wanted to write a novel of "sexual inversion," she consulted Una, Lady Troubridge, her wife, her lover of many years. She thought the book might bring catastrophe, not just to her career, but to their lives. Una replied, "Write what is in your heart … . I wish to be known for what I am and to dwell with you in the palace of truth."

We stroll slowly down the green aisle while I tell you something of what I am writing now, vignettes of daily life, the delicate twining of forbidden words, the way sex and gender and sexuality spread their tendrils through our lives and wrench us open, like the kudzu vine that heaves up asphalt from the road or pulls strands of barbed wire from the fencepost. I tell you how often I am afraid to write what leaps through that gap. As we reach the grape arbor's leafy corridor, you suddenly kneel in front of me and kiss my hands. At the edge of the emerald lawn other visitors stare at the extravagant gesture, while I shift between unease and delight. You say, "I'm telling you now: Whatever you write of me, or of us together, you will never have to ask if I approve. The only place I want to live with you is in the palace of truth."

The night we met, you were first a voice in the dark as you talked about pictures that fell down the slide projector's corridor of light, the faces of people in your history of transgender. One was a photograph of a jazz musician, a handsome white man, square-jawed, looking young for his years. He died of a bleeding ulcer; he could not risk a doctor who might discover he'd been born female. After his death, everyone said that they had no idea. His son said, "He was my dad, the greatest." His wife said, "I never saw him naked. We never had sex. He said something was wrong with him. I never knew." Later I ask you, "Did the wife know?" You say, "Very likely. But then she thought she was the only one. Now her mate is dead, and she is alone with everyone gawking, laughing, pointing their fingers. So of course she would say she didn't know."

Later you tell me of evidence left by other wives, years ago. If the outlaw husband took another lover, sometimes the wife would go to the police and turn her husband in, to be tried, convicted, and sentenced to jail for perversion, the deception of cross-dressing into the opposite sex. Unwittingly, the wife would leave a record, the nakedness of their love between lines in a police report. You say, "But this life is yours and not just mine. You will write a different record of what our life is."

The emergency room nurse is drawing a map for me of this little port town between the river and the salt marshes, halfway down the edge of the South. I am waiting to see a doctor. When the nurse saw you standing next to me, she said,

"Who are you?" When you answered, "Her husband," she said, "Oh, let's put you to work getting these forms filled out." You don't know my social security number. You are afraid they'll ask for a marriage certificate. You've lived so far outside the heterosexual world that I have to tell you, "They *assume*." The white woman at the desk hesitates over your name, gives you the sidelong glance that implies foreigner, alien, Jew. Meanwhile, the nurse treats me like a visiting tourist, recommends the museum by the docks, the old rice mill, the old mansions. It is a town tour of the old slavocracy, but she assumes that's what I want.

She lets you go back with me to a cubicle behind a sliding green curtain. I sit on the gurney, barefoot, naked from the waist up under a flimsy paper gown. I've burned myself badly, hurriedly ironing a dress while I was naked. There is an infected triangle of red printed on the skin of my right breast. I worry that if the doctor thinks you are a man, he will also assume you have abused me. When he comes in, he is short-tempered. You hold my right foot while he handles my breast roughly, implies I'm overreacting, but prescribes a strong antibiotic. He exits, and with him my anxiety that I will lose your presence. He assumed you were a man, and I used the pronoun he expected. This time no one came to stand between us to tell you to leave.

The nurse waves us cheerfully out past her station. She sees us walk away in one dimension while I look back at her from another—alienation. I walk with you down the corridor, and suddenly there are cries. Friends rush a man through. His head lolls, his muddy work pants are stained dark at one thigh. You assess with a glance: a knife wound, but not serious, not enough blood. You stand so calm in the moment's panic that

I see you alone at night in another town, on your feet after another fight, a place where there was more blood. We walk away from the shouting, through the hospital double doors into the humid night.

Behind us, invisible, are the salt marshes, still etched with the ditches of the rice plantations. We know something of the people who once worked knee-deep in water there, caught between the green-speared fences as they grew someone else's food, money, the tissued leaves of rice paper. Before us, by the waterfront, loom lights as tall as an ocean liner, the paper mill of an international company. We know something of the people who work there, who fork green pulpwood into the slurried sulfur-reeking water that becomes brown, white, corrugated, parchment paper. We drive back to our cheap motel by the highway, and I undress. You bandage my breast. You hold me while I rage that I am really married to you. I am with someone in sickness and in health, who holds my torn mortal flesh as dear as her own. Now I will have to find words I have not yet had, the words that creep onto paper and bind my life to you and to this world.

VII.

"THE WAVERING LINE BETWEEN LIGHT AND SHADE ... ."

STRIPPED

The *Times* story is a few inches of words hidden in the back pages of the newspaper I've spread out on our kitchen table. I only notice it because of the headline, the sudden fear that this could almost be you and me: "Woman Who Posed As a Man Is Found Slain With 2 Others." On New Year's Day, Brandon Teena, born a female, living as a man in a small Nebraska town, was murdered, shot in a farmhouse along with the white woman friend he was staying with and a visiting African-American man. Brandon was the only one mutilated with a knife. The week before he had been raped by the two men eventually arrested for his murder. But first, determined to prove he was "really" a woman, they had stripped him at a party, in front of a woman he had dated. Some days earlier the police had decided that his life was a menacing deception. When they'd picked him up on some minor charge and his identification didn't match, the police made sure the town knew he was lying about who he was. But he was clear to his friends: He felt like a man inside; he didn't feel like a woman or a lesbian. He didn't have the money for the operation yet. Within a month he was dead.

When I was a girl, I had a nightmare that still comes back sometimes: *I am standing naked at the center of a circle of people. They laugh at me or point or yell ugly foul words or stare silently. They are clothed. I am stripped down to nothing but my girl's body, and I am ashamed. There is something wrong with me.* I used to think that only women had this nightmare. Now I think everyone dreams of being stripped, but the fingers accuse us of different crimes. People stretch out their hands to show that they know the truth of us better than we do. They strip away our clothes, our words, our skin, our flesh, until we are nothing but a pile of butcher's bones, and then they point and say that is who we are.

I sit in our kitchen and read a *Village Voice* article about the murders. The writer, a lesbian, gleefully gossips with Brandon's ex-girlfriends and repeats salacious details: how "she" fooled them with a dildo, how "she" wouldn't allow touch at breast, thigh, genitals. The writer admits Brandon lived as a man, but she strips him down to prove that he was not. For her, everything has to match—genitals, clothes, pronouns. Besides, how could he be such a good lover of women unless he were a woman? She decides he is a confused lesbian—her kind of lesbian, she writes, a butch woman who turns her on, who gets her hot. The sheriff, who had refused to arrest the rapists when Brandon reported their crime, said, "So far as I'm concerned, you can call it *it*." Throughout the article, the writer calls him *her*: "She was shot execution-style." The writer never mentions he died when he insisted he would choose his own pronoun.

SUNGLASSES

The waiter at the restaurant at water's edge directs us, "Come this way, ladies." And she and she and I follow him into blinding sunlight and sit down at our table with sunglasses firmly on. We've just come from a discussion on gender. One of us jokes that she's heard men can keep their sunglasses on when talking to others, but women won't. Women take off their glasses to be eye to eye with the other. The sun shines on us as if focused through a magnifying lens. We are three tall white women sitting down to lunch, one willowy, one matronly, one elegant. Three women, except two of us have just narrated their stories to the seminar I'm teaching, the story of a metamorphosis older than Ovid, the ancient transformation of male into female. The students were not satisfied with abstraction. They wanted detail, the path mapped out for them. They said to the women: "But what happened to you? How *did* you decide?" Some asked as if the desire to shift sex or gender was strange to them, some because they were looking down that way themselves.

Now we order iced tea, and one of them says, looking right at me, "What is *your* story? How did you get here, to sit down with us?" I tell them about my masculine first girlfriend when I was five, my feminine first husband when I was twenty. I tell of standing as a girl at doors marked *White* and *Colored*, and not knowing what that meant until long after. The long, blindfolded search for the boundaries around me, feeling for the barbed wire called "natural race," "natural gender." I tell of my exhilaration on the summer day every year when I gather with others accused of unnatural acts. We march through the streets searching for freedom, and some men prance like girls, and some women swing their arms like muscle men. The long street of people, hands crossed over and linked in every mixed-up way.

At the end of my story, the sun is so hot on my bent head that my hair feels on fire. I look up at the others and see that one by one, unnoticed, we have laid our dark glasses down, to look at each other with naked eyes.

ART GALLERY

In the art gallery the lighting is discreet but direct on black-and-white pictures. On one side, men, and on the other side, women. But how can we tell which is which? The gallery-goers are trying to look without looking, though looking is what the photographer wants us to do. He shows us himself and others who have not changed into monsters, werewolves, vampires, nor into creatures from a midnight horror show. The men and women are casually at work at a cluttered desk, lounging at home in bed, sitting astride a motorbike. Some are naked and some are clothed.

The artist has photographed himself naked in chiaroscuro, half light, half shadow. He is a slender, not very tall, white man, well-muscled in the shoulders, with a blur of pubic hair. His close-up of his genitals has explanatory text on the transformation of female to male. These are pictures about how small the difference is between *this* and *that*. Sometimes just one chromosome, tossing in its invisible handful of amino acids, nitrogenous bases, sugars, phosphates. Sometimes just the intertwined fingers of hormones, androgen, estrogen, progesterone, sculpting a shape into the body.

Pinpricks of hormones made the difference in your voice, now pitched perfectly between male and female, contralto. I fell in love with your voice first, its deep vibrant tone left from your life as a man. But perhaps I would have left you when your voice altered and your beard grew and your scent changed. You say that, in a way, you are glad you were alone those years you had to figure out what it meant to be a "man." You are glad there was no lover to hurt when you blundered.

But perhaps I would have stayed with you to question what it means to be a "woman." We could have talked night and day about what to keep, what to give away, as we created ourselves in the clear dark.

Perhaps twenty years ago I could not have loved you through all the complications of sex and gender, from woman to man to in-between. But if not, I would have been foolish, to lose you for the sake of such a little difference, the wavering line between light and shade.

BATHROOM

In the middle of farmland, on our way to the Michigan Womyn's Music Festival, we all stop for lunch at McDonald's, stand in line to order fish sandwiches, take turns going to the bathroom. I am last to go and pause between two doors. The signs seem clear, the usual skirt and trouser legs, but suddenly I am confused. How do I choose, given who I've been traveling with?

One companion is a short man with a beard, deep voice, flat chest, who is dressed in trousers, salt-and-pepper half-coat, who was born female, but now lives and functions in every way as a man, a white transsexual man. Another is a tall skinny woman in jeans, with a soft voice and self-deprecating manner, with small breasts under her windbreaker, a woman born male who now lives every day as a woman, a white transsexual lesbian who is taking us to our campsite, the tents and fire pits. And you, in your jeans and black T-shirt, between male and female—you have been in-between all your life.

I can guess you went into the men's room, since you use whichever bathroom is safest at the moment, the one you are least likely to get thrown out of if someone thinks you don't match the picture on the door. I can guess which bathroom was chosen by each of my traveling companions. But after our conversations during the long drive, I feel I could walk through either door. The man, who reminded me of my

199

charming oldest boy cousin, had talked of his earlier job, heavy telephone line work when he had lived as a butch lesbian. He'd talked of his life now as a writer and editor, an organizer for transgender rights. The woman, whose raw energy and verbal patter reminded me of one of my aunts, talked of fearful moments she'd had as she entered bathrooms. There was the father who eyed her as she walked in behind his little girl. Did he suddenly see *pervert?* I said, without saying more that I knew something of that moment of fear: The times I'd stood with clenched hands in a hallway, outside those seemingly simple signs, hoping you would not walk out bloodied from the men's room because someone decided you were too queer to be a "real man." The times I'd stood before the mirror as I washed my hands amid the jostling women, staring at myself as grotesque, someone I could not recognize as a "real woman."

I waver between the two signs. The last restaurant I was in had opposite doors with plaster masks. One, a blank smooth face with streaming hair, was beautiful as a cover-girl model, presumably a woman. The other was a face that gnashed its teeth and grinned, a satyr, a devil, presumably a man. The signs tell me clearly what the problem is: Not whose genitals are where, but what values we attach to them. Today the signs present my choices—*Skirt* or *Trousers.* We haven't yet reached our destination, a transgendered encampment outside the gates of women's land. There, everyone waits to discover the other through what people choose to reveal of their sex and gender. But here, I have only two choices. In my sandals and well-worn jeans, I push open the door that says *Skirt.*

BORDER

At the campsite outside women's land, a lesbian femme talks to me about her decision to come to the music festival. She was reluctant after she heard a transsexual lesbian had been thrown out the previous year, accused of being a man. Still, this was a vacation they could afford, just barely. So she told her butch—who didn't look like someone who could pass the "woman-born-woman only" policy—that she would drive them in. Maybe the women at the gate would be less likely to notice them because as a femme, she looked the way people expected a woman to look. The rumor was that the transsexual woman could have stayed last year, if she'd been willing to strip. The femme didn't want her butch to have to go through that.

I remembered how you and I rehearsed what we would say at the border, going into Canada, coming back to the U.S. You drove through; the guard would expect the husband to be driving. We dressed up, professionals on our way to a "writer's workshop." We didn't mention the books in the trunk, the ones that we'd written, on an official list to be seized at the border as pornography. We were very careful; you'd been stopped here before. And there were the queer friends who'd been pulled over, strip-searched, sent back. The activists whose cars were taken apart piece by piece and searched. The Six Nations women, the African-American women, strip-searched and held with their children for hours. As we drove up to the guard, I took off my sunglasses and smiled engagingly. You casually rested your wedding ring on the window's edge. We gritted our teeth and thought about all the reasons a nation-state regulates sex and gender and race and class. It was not for our protection that the police stared at us so fixedly before he waved us through.

At the gates of women's land, volunteers wave the cars and campers through to a place that is certainly no nation, just a summer haven for a few thousand women and a temporary town that is also a profitable business for its owners. But when we ask, the women at the gate can't tell us exactly what kind of women are welcome. Does the policy of woman-born-woman mean that if you are born a female you are always a woman? Then the member of the group who is a female-to-male transsexual should be able to come in, though he makes it plain that he doesn't want to. As a man, he respects the boundaries of women's space. But the male-to-female transsexual, who always felt herself to be a girl and was frequently called one by taunting boys, says, "I am a woman. I belong here." Another woman asks about her status as someone who was born with an ambiguity of male and female genitals. She was raised to be a woman, she lives as a lesbian. The gate-keepers hesitate. She asks, "Can only *half* of me come in?" Finally, you identify yourself as a butch lesbian. You speak of your transgendered existence between woman and man, born female, but male in gender expression. You explain that you can't always live openly as a transgendered person, that you and I sometimes pass as husband and wife for safety. When you ask if you'd be welcome on women's land, at first the gate-keeper says, "We'd prefer you didn't come in."

The last and only time I'd been at the festival, I'd walked uneasily around the temporary town of six thousand or so women, on paths that wound between tents, performance stages, and masses of ferns. This women's land, this refuge, felt unreal and dangerous to me. Finally, after walking by thousands and thousands of white women, I realized I'd never lived, even briefly, in a place that had so few people of color. The only space I'd occupied for any length of time that was more segregated was the whites-only schoolroom of my childhood.

Now, ten years later, I find that to be admitted here I and the other women have to pass a biological test: Are you a pure, natural-born woman? Surely I can't be the only one who fears a sisterhood based on biological definitions, the kind that have been used in the larger world to justify everything from job discrimination (because women have smaller brains and aren't as smart) to hysterectomies (because women's wombs make us hysterical). And I can't be the only one who grew up trained into the cult of pure white womanhood and heard biological reasons given to explain actions against people of color, everything from segregation of water fountains to lynching. If this gathering of women in the dusty fields beyond the gate is a community based on biological purity, then it offers me, a "real woman," no real safety.

At the front gate, the questioners are still asking the gate-keepers how they can be so sure of the boundaries of womanhood. It seems that anyone with experience in a male body need not apply, since they would be prone to violence. I wonder how many of the women who pass through these gates actually believe that any person born in a woman's body inevitably knows how to be kind and fair? Eventually, after many phone calls to higher-ups, the gatekeepers say they will admit, though perhaps only for today, anyone who self-identifies as a *woman-born-woman*—if, of course, these people have the money to pay for admission.

Inside the festival, after our group is invited to a workshop organized by the Lesbian Avengers, a lively discussion continues between women campers and those of us from Camp Trans. Suddenly a white woman approaches and says with outrage, "I was walking by here and felt boy energy, then I saw you. I came here to be with women only. You don't belong here." She is speaking to someone who she has selected as transsexual because of the slogan on her T-shirt. You turn to the angry woman and ask quietly, "What about me? Do I have male energy? Am I a woman or a man?" She pauses, taken aback, and finally says, "I don't want to talk about each person …" You reply, "But you do want someone to decide. You want someone to judge, and us to submit to judgment. So tell me, am I a man or a woman? Tell me how *you* can decide." The woman falls completely silent; all of us sit silent. She does not answer. She walks away.

Later our group walks back through the festival to our camp across the road. We look no different from the other white women who are milling around us along the crowded paths. But we include transgender, pre-operative, post-op and non-op transsexual, crossdressing, biological, cultural, butch, femme, and unclassifiable women. An African-American woman, partying in front of her tent, sees us on our impromptu march. She yells, "I don't know what you're walking for, but—*go girls!*"

Other women are applauding, but I'm ready to leave. Perhaps I've been too long inside the "culture of womanhood," trying to expand who that includes. I miss the words *women's liberation*. I want to fight women's oppression, not make a place in which I can *be* "woman." Still, as we walk out the long dusty road to the gate, I flinch at the women who stare, and dread the disapproval of those who will say I have forfeited my place as a "real woman," a "real lesbian."

As we walk through the festival, we look much like the other women, and we sound like them. In brief wisps of talk, we tell the experiences we share with them: The post-op transsexual woman raped repeatedly in her childhood by her father when he saw her as an effeminate little boy. The butch lesbian verbally abused by her parents because she was "too masculine" for a girl child and couldn't change how she walked. The femme lesbian sexually harassed on the street because she wouldn't smile when a man asked her to. The pre-op transsexual woman who lost custody of the children she had fathered, who said over and over, "My babies." The women who supported themselves working as a waitress, or a secretary, or on the factory assembly line, and then lost their jobs when the companies fired "surplus workers." The woman who lost her job because someone "outed" her to her boss as transsexual. The non-op women who used their bodies any way they had to in order to pay the rent, turning tricks with men on the street. The woman beaten, stabbed on the street because somehow her body seemed "wrong." The stories, the terrible stories, different and yet like the stories I've heard women tell for years. Each of us coming to womanhood from inside the living of our own stories.

I stand on the sandy road that runs between the two en-campments, at the boundary of womanhood. I don't want *woman* to be a fortress that has to be defended. I want it to be a life we constantly braid together from the threads of our existence, a rope we make, a flexible weapon stronger than steel, that we use to pull down walls that imprison us at the borders.

PROFITS

On the first anniversary of the Montreal massacre, I tell my feminist theory class about the moment when a man with a rifle entered an engineering class at that university. He divided the students up, men to one wall, women to the other. When he had decided who was male and who was female, he shot the women, killing fourteen of them. Later he said he wanted the women dead because they were feminists and were taking jobs away from men. I say that there is no record of how many, if any, of the women considered themselves feminists. Perhaps they were just women who wanted to work in a job designated *male* in this century, on this continent. I say crossing gender boundaries as women does not automatically make us feminists, but the consequences of doing so may, if we live.

During the discussion, a student raises her hand. At a women's music festival last summer, she had met a survivor of the massacre. The woman had lived because the male terrorist had perceived her as male and put her in the group with the men. Although my student, who herself looks like a teenage boy, doesn't recount how the woman felt watching the other women die, her face is blotched and etched with anguish. I imagine that room: The woman facing a man so sure he knows who is *man* and who is *woman*. His illusion of omniscience spares her, allows her to become an engineer, and then she spends years trying to find work. She gets turned down for jobs as "too masculine" if she is seen as woman, "too effeminate" if seen as man. To the students I say there is no gender boundary that can make us into either one or the other. There is no method, including violence, that can enforce complete conformity to "man," to "woman." I say we know that this man hated women, that he meant to kill women, but what we do not know is how many ways of being human have been hidden in the word *woman*. We don't yet know how large is this *other* that has been made the opposite of the narrow rod of *man*. We don't know who was male or female in that Montreal room, how many genders lived or died. I say that *here* we are trying to end a war on women in which we all get caught in the crossfire.

In this basement classroom, the steam pipes crisscross the ceiling and drip on our heads. Other students on campus bait those who take this women's studies course—the men are called feminine, the women masculine, the men queer, the women dykes. They are seen as crossing sex and gender boundaries simply because they question them. Today we all jump at noises in the hall, imagining that the one we fear stands in the doorway. Perhaps an unknown man, perhaps someone from our family with a cold, murderous stare. The ones who believe the lie that there are only men and women, and that the first should rule the last. The ones who believe we should keep separate, sheep and goats, until judgment day. It is 3:30 p.m., the end of today's class. I assign readings on the origin of the family, private property, women, and the State. I say, "Next time we will talk about gender stratification and corporate profit."

STONE HOME

Above Times Square, huge words run glittering across the walls of buildings, and we walk underneath, holding hands anonymously. We walk away from the Broadway Theater, toward the subway, toward home. The streets still run wet from a thunderstorm that rocked the stage just before the brass walls fell clanging down and Medea stretched out her bloody hands, defiant murderer of her children. I want to joke that she was then what the Christian Right says I am now: a woman who left her husband and annihilated her children, who practices witchcraft and wants to destroy capitalism, a woman who has turned into a lesbian. But she reminds me more of myself as a young bride, when with my husband, I entered, unwitting, the home I thought of as ours.

When I crossed that threshold, I entered a house whose foundation depended on my docile hands, my laying it in place every day, act after act, brick after brick, walling myself in. The house as mausoleum, as sarcophagus. The house where one foundation corner rested on the body of the white women who never said No to the men who owned the place. When I stood up and left, there was a screaming of walls, like the shriek of torn metal. There were the silent voices of women I heard screaming. My voice screaming. I thought I would go mad when my children were taken. I thought they would die without me and I without them. Where was the land where

209

they could be with me, where women, men, and children were no one's possession? I went to the other women, clenched angry groups in courtyards, on the streets, chanting. I became a lover of women and without a home. I launched myself, errant, on a long journey to a place that does not yet exist.

Now I am on this strange street with you, in a place where the sky flashes with the names of those who own the city, written in letters bigger than houses. I live with you here where the ground shakes with the machinery of money, where people are ground up for profit, their lives pulverized to bonemeal between millstones. We clamber down the steps to the subway, say, "Good evening" to the man who works on the first landing, panhandling. My fingers search my pocket for coins. At the bottom of the stairs we wait on the platform. We watch the other travelers, uneasy, trying to place us as *man*, *woman*, into some opposition. Uneasy, we watch the travelers, trying to place them as danger, ally. On the train, a woman walks through the cars singing a song about love, for money.

As the train emerges from underground, I see that the granite walls__ of the tunnel are held together with huge iron bolts. I see the lights of the office buildings, the bank buildings, perched above the tunnel. We walk home talking again of fundamental change, of the edifice of what is to be done. We are the obscure stones at whose shift the walls will crack from bottom to top, dirt to wind, so that all can be built again for all. If the lowest stones move, those who scrape and sell even the sky will crash down in a scatter of glittering rock.

ACKNOWLEDGEMENTS

For wonderful and lively conversations I've had about the ideas dealt with in this book, many thanks to Dorothy Allison, Judith Arcana, Evelyn Torton Beck, Chrystos, Jewelle Gomez, Biddy Martin, Adrienne Rich, and Imani Woody.

Much appreciation for their insights to the participants in the Union Institute "Gender Blending/Bending/Breaking" seminar, especially Marcia Botzer, Licia Fiol-Matta, Aurora Levins Morales, and Becky Logan. I am also very grateful to those organizing and attending the 1994 Camps Trans, especially Riki Ann Wilchins and James Green.

For her years of friendship and her invaluable editorial advice, I thank Elly Bulkin. Heartfelt thanks to Nanette Gartrell, Holly Hughes, Dee Mosbacher, Ben Weaver, and Ransom Weaver for friendship and loving support. Overdue thanks to Kate Clinton for the long-ago use of her apartment as a writing retreat. And to Joanie Brindisi: bless you for all those next steps.

My deepest thanks, once again, to Nancy K. Bereano, for her continued belief in my work, and for her skillful, dedicated editing.

Leslie Feinberg has given me inspiration, creative editing, theoretical collaboration, and unstinting love. Thank you, Leslie, for being at the heart of this book and at the heart of my life.

The writing of this book was made possible in part by a grant from the National Endowment for the Arts.

A NOTE ABOUT LANGUAGE

Prior to the republication of *S/HE*, Minnie Bruce Pratt wanted to write a brief statement about language and her use of pronouns in the book. She did not complete that task before she died.

In *S/HE*, Minnie Bruce Pratt bridges being part of two vital movements: women's liberation and transgender liberation. While composing the book in the early 1990s, Pratt wrote with the languages she had, working existing words to develop new languages to express the experiences and intricacies of sex and gender realities as she experienced and observed them.

Minnie Bruce Pratt wrote on Leslie Feinberg's website (www.LeslieFeinberg.net):

> In a statement at the end of hir life, Leslie said zie/ she had "never been in search of a common umbrella identity, or even an umbrella term, that brings together people of oppressed sexes, gender expressions, and sexualities" and added that she/zie believed in the right of self-determination for oppressed individuals, communities, groups, and nations.

This edition retains the language from its original publication in 1995. Of course, Minnie Bruce Pratt's thinking and language about gender, sex, gender identity, and sexuality evolved, changed, and continued to grow after the publication of this book. We hope that readers will engage *S/HE* and its language in the spirit of respect that it was written and that readers will hear and imagine words that speak them into affirmative existence.

Leslie preferred to use the pronouns she/zie and her/hir for hirself, but also said:

"I care which pronoun is used, but people have been respectful to me with the wrong pronoun and disrespectful with the right one. It matters whether someone is using the pronoun as a bigot, or if they are trying to demonstrate respect."

—Julie R. Enszer

DISCUSSION QUESTIONS

1. What themes appear in the text? (e.g. fluidity, flexibility, boundaries, borders...) What metaphors and motifs do you notice in the text? (e.g. skin/surface, fabric/touch, soft/stiff, interior/exterior...)
2. What role do different kinds of love and loving play throughout the book? What is the radical potential of love?
3. Where do you see desire, shame, care, or transformation appear and intersect in *S/HE?* What roles are played by place, body, and memory? What is the role of location, especially the South, in this book?
4. How does Pratt describe the development of her sensuousness, desire, and sexuality? And why are these dimensions of her life important? What other senses does she engage or describe, from the smell of skin to the charge of brief eye contact?
5. How do erotic experiences intersect with experiences we might otherwise call political? Where do the erotic and the political intersect or overlap in the book?
6. What do genre, style, and form in *S/HE* contribute to Pratt's reflections on gender and sexuality? How are the parts (I, II, III...) organized? Is it by time, theme, or another dimension? How do the titles shape your understanding of how Pratt reflects on and organizes her thoughts?
7. What patterns do you see across titles within the parts, or across multiple parts, uniting or contrasting chapters?

Where do you see Pratt repeating language or concepts in different pieces, and how are these echoed moments used in their different chapters?

8. This book was published in 1995. Where do you see overlaps with our current moment? Where did you find yourself surprised or challenged by the socio-cultural-political moment and time periods described in the text? Did you read any chapter and just think, "this is not possible today?" What has changed, or what surprised you, about what was/is possible?

9. Throughout the book the speaker and Leslie Feinberg are constantly negotiating visibility and legibility. How do you understand the descriptions of queer/trans* visibility as political acts in the 1990s versus the politics of queer/trans* visibility today?

10. What can trans*/GNC/non-binary people, feminists, and activists learn from reading S/HE?

11. What do you think Pratt means when she writes: "I say crossing gender boundaries as women does not automatically make us feminists, but the consequences of doing so may, if we live."?

12. How are gender and capitalism connected according to Pratt? What steps have we made towards "a liberation movement that offered both gender freedom and the end of capitalism" and how might we continue on that path?

13. How does Pratt engage with intersectionality? How does Pratt think about difference?

14. What is the relationship between theory, praxis, and bodies in S/HE? How does Pratt understand theory? What can we learn from theory, and what are its limitations? What are ways we can give theory flesh and breath? What

does it mean to put the book to use in this way, as instructive?

15. Consider some of the below questions posed by Minnie Bruce Pratt.

"No one had turned to us and held out a handful of questions: **How many ways are there to have the *sex* of girl, boy, man, woman? How many ways are there to have *gender*—from masculine to androgynous to feminine? Is there a connection between the *sexualities* of lesbian, bisexual, heterosexual, between desire and liberation?** No one told us: The path divides, and divides again, in many directions. No one asked: **How many ways can the *body's sex* vary by chromosomes, hormones, genitals? How many ways can *gender expression* multiply—between home and work, at the computer and when you kiss someone, in your dreams and when you walk down the street?** No one asked us: **What is your dream of who you want to be?**"

16. What is Pratt's critique of reform politics and how might we learn from it?

17. How does Pratt attend to contradictions? How does gender both constrain us and have the potential to liberate us?

18. What do you think Pratt means by this: "Now I say, 'A femme is not a woman, at least not the woman people think. It's a case of mistaken identity.'" What does the category/identity/word woman mean for Pratt? How does femmephobia show up in this text, and today?

19. Pratt writes about "deep fear in the larger culture, and therefore within ourselves, about sex and gender fluidity." How does this fear still appear to us today? What can we

do to combat and ease this fear? What pathways or strategies are you getting from Pratt's text to address this fear and its oppressive repercussions?

20. How do "gender oppression and liberation affect everyone"?

21. Choose a specific event or location you did not recognize that Pratt refers to in the text, e.g. Michfest or the news story in "Penis," and learn about it. How do you understand the chapter differently now that you have a better understanding of the context?

Developed by Taylor Marie Doherty in consultation with Julie Enszer, Elizabeth Venell and E.R. Anderson.

Taylor Marie Doherty M.A. (she/they) is a PhD Student in Gender and Women's Studies at the University of Arizona with PhD minors in Information and Social, Cultural, and Critical Theory. Their interdisciplinary research and teaching interests include political theory, Black feminist theory, queer & trans* studies, transnational feminisms, social movements, community archives, archival theory and praxis, and cultural studies. Beyond academia Taylor is a labor organizer, translator, amateur herbalist, and poet from Boston, Massachusetts.

Sinister Wisdom
A Multicultural Lesbian Literary & Art Journal

Sinister Wisdom is a multicultural lesbian literary & art journal that publishes four issues each year. Publishing since 1976, *Sinister Wisdom* works to create a multicultural, multi-class lesbian space. *Sinister Wisdom* seeks to open, consider, and advance the exploration of community issues. *Sinister Wisdom* recognizes the power of language to reflect our diverse experiences and to enhance our ability to develop critical judgment, as lesbians evaluating our community and our world.

Editor and Publisher: Julie R. Enszer, PhD

Former editors and publishers:
Harriet Ellenberger (aka Desmoines)
and Catherine Nicholson (1976–1981)
Michelle Cliff and Adrienne Rich (1981–1983)
Michaele Uccella (1983–1984)
Melanie Kaye/Kantrowitz (1983–1987)
Elana Dykewomon (1987–1994)
Caryatis Cardea (1991–1994)
Akiba Onada-Sikwoia (1995–1997)
Margo Mercedes Rivera-Weiss (1997–2000)
Fran Day (2004–2010)
Julie R. Enszer & Merry Gangemi (2010–2013)

Subscribe online: www.SinisterWisdom.org

Sinister Wisdom is a U.S. nonprofit organization; donations to support the work and distribution of *Sinister Wisdom* are welcome and appreciated.

Sapphic Classic

Sapphic Classics are reprint editions of iconic works of lesbian writing, or new works, from influential lesbian writers. Inaugurated in 2013 with *Crime Against Nature* by Minnie Bruce Pratt, the Sapphic Classics series brings important collections of lesbian writing back into print, making them available to reach new readers.

Other Titles in the Sapphic Classics Series include:

Crime Against Nature by Minnie Bruce Pratt
Living as a Lesbian by Cheryl Clarke
What Can I Ask:
    New and Selected Poems 1975-2014 by Elana Dykewomon
The Complete Works of Pat Parker
Sister Love: The Letters of Audre Lorde and Pat Parker
    1974-1989
For the Hard Ones: A Lesbian Phenomenology
    by tatiana de la tierra
A Generous Spirit: Selected Work by Beth Brant
Eruptions of Inanna by Judy Grahn
A Sturdy Yes of a People: Selected Writings by Joan Nestle
Fire-Rimmed Eden: Selected Poems by Lynn Lonidier
The Highest Apple: Sappho and the Lesbian Poetic Tradition
by Judy Grahn